TOUGH TALK

TOUGH TALK

True Stories of East London Hard Men

**ARTHUR WHITE, STEVE JOHNSON
AND IAN MCDOWALL**
with
MILLIE MURRAY

**Authentic
LIFESTYLE**

TOUGH TALK

Copyright © 2000 Millie Murray & Tough Talk

First published 2000.
This edition published by Authentic Lifestyle,
an imprint of Authentic Media,
9 Holdom Avenue, Bletchley, Milton Keynes,
Bucks, MK1 1QR, UK.

3 4 5 6 7   08 07 06 05 04 03

ISBN 1-86024-378-9

All Scripture quotations are from the
New King James Version © 1979, 1980, 1982
Thomas Nelson Publishers, Inc.

British Library Cataloguing-in-Publication Data
A catalogue record for this book is
available from the British Library.

Produced for Authentic Lifestyle by
Bookprint Creative Services, P.O. Box 827, BN21 3YJ, England.
Printed in Great Britain.

This book is dedicated to

Jacqui, Emma and James White,
without whose love and understanding,
Arthur wouldn't have been able to
get through the tough times.

The Johnson family, especially Lisa,
who has seen Steve at his worst – and best!

Valerie and Bianca McDowall,
and to Ian's mum and sister and brothers,
for their love and support.

CONTENTS

Author's Note

Some of the names and places referred to in these stories have been changed to protect people involved.

FOREWORD

For the past few years I have had the privilege of knowing these three men. I have worked closely with them, and have heard them speak countless times about the dramatic changes that have taken place in their lives.

From drugs, alcohol, violence and immoral relationships they have been able, not only to overcome and endure the harshness of their lives, but now they dedicate their time to telling people that they don't have to remain in that state.

Having worked with these guys, in many different situations, I have been impressed with their integrity, honesty and the motives that drive them on. The world that they used to inhabit was dark and dangerous. Readers may find some of their experiences shocking to read. However, within each story lies the same inspiring message of hope.

The hope that these men have is available to everyone. No matter what your background or lifestyle is: all it takes is listening ears and an open mind.

Their stories are truly remarkable, and deserve to be widely read and told.

Pastor Sean O'Boyle, Powerhouse Church, Wood Green, London

ARTHUR WHITE

Chapter 1

CHAMPION OF THE WORLD!

'Ladies and Gentlemen, the European and World Heavyweight Champion of 1992, from Great Britain, Arthur White.'

The applause was deafening. Walking towards the rostrum with the sound of the crowd in my ears, I felt myself swelling up, ready to burst. As I drew alongside the MC, out of the corner of my mouth, I said to him: 'Would yer say that again?'

'Ladies and Gentlemen, the . . .'

His words puffed me up even more. By the time I reached the rostrum I felt that I had added ten foot to my six foot frame. This was what life was all about for me – winning – coming first.

Swaggering across the platform, I raised my hand to acknowledge my followers who were still clapping. Up on the rostrum the applause sounded like thunder. I lifted my hands and turned from side to side. Flashes of light from photographers, and the bright light from TV cameras, boosted my ego again. This was the 'ultimate' for me. The pinnacle of my sixteen years as an international athlete. I bent my head to receive the medal that Keiron Stanley, President of the British Power-lifting Organisation, placed over my head. In fact, that evening I picked up no less than five medals: European Champion, European Best Lifter, World Champion, runner-up World Best Lifter, British Power-lifting Hall of Fame.

After the awards ceremony, I was still riding high from the whole day's events. People came up to congratulate me, slapping me on the back, shaking my hand, 'Well done mate.' 'Good lifting.' 'I knew yer'd win.' 'Still the best.'

The tee-shirt that I was wearing confirmed what had happened to me that night, and what my fans were saying: 'There Can Be Only One.' I wanted the evening to go on forever. A few of the Lifters and some of the boys decided to meet up later.

To get out of the Forum took forever. It seemed like people were popping up all over the place, just to have a few words with me, and wanting my autograph. I savoured the praise, but I could sense that it was time for me to get back to my hotel room.

I managed to manoeuvre myself out of the door. With the crowds behind me, I could focus now on the evening ahead. My mood was slowly shifting into a downward mode. I knew what was happening – and I knew the answer to remedy it.

As soon as I set foot into my hotel room, I made a beeline for the bathroom. There, on the shelf was my toilet bag. Quickly unzipping the bag, I pulled out the small paper envelope. My heart began to beat faster, as I greedily and carefully unfolded the paper. Throwing the wash bag to one side, I emptied the gram of cocaine into a line onto the glass shelf. Straightening the envelope out, I then rolled it up, and used it as a straw to snort up the powder. The initial feeling of relief was soon followed by the fast surge of adrenaline, pumping through my veins. By the time I got under the shower, I felt that I was invincible. It seemed as though somebody else was on the inside of me who wanted to come out. Every fibre of my being was pulsating. I couldn't keep still – I had to get out. It seemed that within the space of five minutes, I was washed, dressed and out the door, looking for more action.

In the foyer, I met up with some of the other guys, and as the cabs came rolling up to the front door, we took it in turns to pile in. The effects of the cocaine were really kicking in. My mouth was going thirteen to the dozen. It was a tight squeeze with four other 'lifters' in a cab. I couldn't keep still. I was eager to get to the nightclub.

I didn't have a clue as to where we were going, or what the club was called, but as the cab drew up outside, I felt my mood swing up a couple of notches. The bright lights, and the crowd of people that were hanging about outside, made me impatient to get in.

The atmosphere inside the club was intoxicating. I had brought some more coke with me, just in case. The heavy rhythmic beat captivated my senses. I felt as though the whole of me was taken over by a force – which I wasn't fighting – in fact I was quite happy to be led by the coke, the beer and the hypnotic effects of the club. I couldn't really hear myself think, and to be truthful I didn't want to think about my life, and what was reality. The here and now was what I was living for.

The music had me swinging my $16^1/_2$-stone bulk all over the place – John Travolta had nothing on me that night. There were some young dancers up on the podiums throughout the club, giving it all they had. My mates and I were laughing at them. Then, one of my friends said, 'Ere Arfer, you can do better than that.' Grinning, I didn't need to be asked twice. I tore off my jacket, and also ripped off my shirt in my haste to get up there. The guy whose spot I took didn't have time to register what was happening to him. I pushed him out of the way, and got down into some serious movements. I thought I was on *Top of the Pops*. I danced, non-stop for a while, and I would have continued, had the doorman not come along and told me to get down. The way I was feeling, I knew that I could have easily sorted him out. But it wasn't worth it. I was out for a good time, not for trouble. Anyway, no-one could beat me, so I thought it was time for another beer.

The night wore on all too quickly. Before I knew it, it was time to go. The other guys wanted to go back to the hotel, but I could have stayed for much longer. We left.

Back in my room, the sad truth of my life caught up with me.

The curtains were drawn, and the side lamp cast an eerie glow, which matched my mood. The coke and booze had worn off. The mask that I had upheld throughout the day was gone. This was the real me. The nightmare that I was living had now come home to haunt me. Sitting in the armchair, I held my head in my hands and wept. This should have been a time of celebration. My wife and kids should have been with me, sharing in my victory. Instead, I was a broken mess. My hard, steel-like exterior, was one great big lie. I was a lonely man.

Empty of drugs, my mind whirled and somersaulted over different times in my life: at home with my wife Jacqui, having a meal; in the garden, laughing and joking; playing around with my two kids, Emma and James. It all seemed so unreal now, miles and miles away from them, not only in distance, but in love, in everyday contact. Resting my head back against the armchair, I wondered what it was all about – my life.

Tears streamed down my eyes, blinding my vision. The pain of my sobbing was cutting into every part of me. My chest felt sore, with all the heaving and deep emotion that I was experiencing. Now, would be the time, I thought to end it all. No more pain for my wife and kids. I too, would be free from this suffering. Bending down, I unstrapped the twelve-inch diver's knife from my left leg. I rested it on the small table in front of me. The black handled, shiny silver knife seemed to draw me closer to it. Something was pulling my hand, to pick up the knife. It would be so simple – one slash across my throat – the end. Beads of sweat trickled down my forehead. The air felt oppressive, and it felt hard to breathe. One cut. Quick. Painless. My eyelids were like sheets of lead. I was perspiring all over. My mind was spinning around like a carousel, out of control. My mind went blank. I felt myself falling into oblivion.

The next thing I knew, the pale November morning light was streaming through a gap in the curtains. It was an effort for me to get up. My mind groggily began to get into focus, as I stretched my body. My muscles ached. My brain ached. Gingerly, I walked over to the patch of floor, where I had thrown my jacket the night before. I fished the small envelope out, and started to prepare myself for another rush.

* * *

Mr Sethers, the gym master at Fairmead Secondary School, had told my fourth form class, that if anyone wanted to be selected for the school athletics team, they had to stay after school for the trials. I didn't have to be asked twice. At fourteen, I enjoyed sports more than anything. My speciality was sprinting. I had represented the school on a few occasions, and I knew that this would be no different. I was eager and anticipated my selection. Mr Sethers had a bit of a soft spot for me. He was always encouraging me to do better, which boosted my confidence, and increased my competitiveness. Wanting to do well, in whatever I did, especially sports, was something that I think I must have been born with.

With my hands on the white line, and my feet on the starting block, I was poised, ready to shoot off towards the winning line. I won the 100 metres. I usually did. I went on to become the West Essex Junior Champion, Essex Junior Champion, and I equalled the 100 metres national record, all before I was sixteen.

Living on the Debden council estate, in Loughton, Essex was great for a boy like me. The sprawling estate was surrounded by acres and acres of grass verges, fields, and it bordered Epping Forest. To be able to take a short walk from my house, and find myself in a chest-high field of corn, was heaven for me. It was a stark contrast to the war-torn East End I knew as a young child. In those days, it was safe for children to go out alone, without fear of being abducted.

At home, my Dad was the head of the house, and what he said went. But, it was my Mum that I shared my innermost thoughts with. She was the one who supported me in all that I did.

It was around this time that I started to train with weights. At first, it was because I just wanted to build up more muscle for running. But, as my body developed, and I felt good about myself, I realised, that I was going to leave behind the running, and stick with the weightlifting.

Not only was I aware of my body changing, but I also began to pay attention to the opposite sex. I met my wife Jacqui, when we were both fourteen. From the time I clapped eyes on her, I knew she was the one for me. I was sitting on the wall of the pub – The Gunmakers, in Loughton – when I saw her, my heart skipped a beat, and I suddenly felt shy. I would have married her then if I could, but, I was prepared to bide my time.

I left school in 1968. Being 17 years old, I felt that I wanted to conquer the world. I was eager to earn money. I wanted to, and knew that I was going to be successful at whatever I turned my hands to. In fact, being very good with my hands I became an apprentice carpenter and joiner. C. S. Foster & Sons, was a great firm to work for: I came into my own once I started working for them. Being the youngest worker, I was taken under the wing of the older men, and shown the ropes. I grew up quickly, picking up tips on working skills and life.

By 1972, I was fully qualified. I felt able to face the world and all that it had to offer. Jacqui and I had married the previous year. Life for me was good – I had become a man. It was a great feeling and the need for me to be in control of every area of my life propelled me into becoming self-employed. Don't get me wrong – I love working with other people – but the time had come for me to branch out on my own.

Any feelings of apprehension that I had in starting up my own business, were soon quelled. The building industry was booming. Money was not in short supply. Being prepared to work hard didn't go unnoticed, and soon contracts were coming in from all over the place. It seemed that I was working from morning to night. I had to, because I reasoned to myself that I had to make as much money as I could while I had my health and strength. I had picked the right woman for my wife, because Jacqui wasn't my partner only at home, she worked right alongside me too – we were very close.

My love for Jacqui grew almost daily: she was like a part of my body; our minds were so alike; we were inseparable. Never, could I envisage a time when we would ever be apart. When friends or workmates were talking about women other than their wives, or whistling at women walking along the road, I didn't join in. It was alien to my thoughts to want to be with another woman, whether in mind or deed.

During these early years of my working life, for leisure, I would go to the gym. This was purely for my own pleasure. I loved training. It was a wind-down for me. There, I was free from the pressures of life. It was a time to clear my mind, and help keep my body fit and strong.

Wag Bennett's gym was a very popular and well-known gym. It was frequented by all the top body builders from all over the world. Arnold Schwartzenegger was a friend of Wag's and a regular visitor to the gym.

I loved preening myself in the mirrors around the gym walls. My body was shaping up nicely, and my muscles were honing up to perfection. The strength that I was gaining was not just limited to superficial muscle. I had tendon strength, which is innate. It's a strength that cannot be acquired – you either have it or you don't. My skeletal frame was also strong, and this enabled me to carry the extra weight.

Deep within myself I also knew that I was strong. My mind would create scenarios that had me battling against the odds: being involved in a train crash where I would not only survive, but, would be a human crane in lifting up the wreckage to save people's lives. Or perhaps I would be involved in a horrific car accident and my body would be pierced by a long piece of metal, but I would yank it out and to the amazement of those around me, I would get up and walk away. I had convinced myself that I was invincible.

At about this time, I met up with a guy called George Manners. He used the gym and he was a coach at the Bethnal Green Weightlifting Club. George invited me to join his club. He had been watching me, over a period of time as I trained, and felt that I had something to offer.

At the Bethnal Green club, I felt that I had come home. Most of my family had originated from East London, and training with the guys there, was like being among my family. George was my mentor. He was a disciplinarian. He had taken part in the 1964 Olympics and had won many competitions. He taught me the correct procedures for weightlifting, and how to discipline myself. He worked me very hard, but, it was something that I really enjoyed. He could see that I was eager, and in 1975 he encouraged me to become an instructor.

The instructor's course was being held at Bisham Abbey in Oxfordshire, which is the British National Sport Centre, where all the England squads train, in every sport. Whilst there, I met up with Ron Reeves. He owned his own gym in Sittingbourne, Kent and had his own team of weightlifters that would compete in competitions around the country. He asked me whether I fancied lifting for him at the weekends.

Entering competitions had never really been one of my goals. I was more comfortable with the idea of instructing, but when Ron asked me, I considered his proposition. He had obviously been watching me throughout the weekend, and felt that I would be an asset to the team. It didn't take me long to make up my mind that I would give it a crack. I knew I was strong and could handle it, so, I told him I would.

I lifted weights for Ron's team from 1975 until 1979. During this time, I had a number of successes: I won the Kent Championships three years running; I won the South East Counties

Championships; the Home Counties Championships; Bronze Medal in the British Championships; and Bronze Medal in the World Championships which were held in the USA. Throughout this period also, I broke a number of British, European and Commonwealth records, and continued to win many smaller domestic competitions.

After six years of marriage, my beautiful daughter Emma was born. Jacqui and I had not really thought about having children, we were having such a good time with each other and with our individual interests. But having Emma was an added bonus.

My business continued to grow, reaching new heights all the time. 1980 was a great year: my son and heir, James, was born and this was truly the 'icing on the cake' for Jacqui and I; our family felt complete.

Although I was having the time of my life, I knew that life for my wife was hard. She had two small children to look after, as well as running the house. Jacqui still found time to help me as much as she could with the business, and she fully supported me in my weightlifting career. Nevertheless, it was a difficult time for her, but as the children grew up, Jacqui was released more and more to do the things she wanted to do.

In 1980, I gained a silver medal in the European Champion-ships, second place at the British Championships, and a Bronze Medal at the World Championships. Then in 1981, I kicked off big time. I was now a regular member of the British Team. I was representing Britain all over the world: USA, Hawaii, Italy, Switzerland, Finland, Germany, India, Holland and France. I felt as though I had become an international globetrotter. Wherever I went throughout the globe, I was heralded as a celebrity. My entering a competition, caused my competitors to fear. They knew that I would be on form, and that my one intention was to win a Gold, Silver, or Bronze medal at least. I was no time waster! The adoration that I received made me feel powerful. To say I felt more than human, bordering on super-human, wouldn't be an understatement.

Coming home brought me back down to earth. Initially, having my photo in the papers, attending parties, and riding on the wave of my successes, and all that these entailed was great. But soon, reality hit home. Back to work, paying the bills, being a loving husband and father, and training at the gym, sobered me up. Yet, hankering after the trappings of success grew and grew. It was as though something was awakened within me, that had to be fed. Its food was winning.

I won the 1981 British Championships; the European Championships and I came second in the World Championships. I continued breaking records along the way. I was a force to be reckoned with – nothing could stop me.

In 1982, business was booming and I met a man who was Chairman of a group of companies. He gave me a big contract to convert warehouses and offices in Harlow and it made sense for me to move my whole business to Harlow, where my wife continued to do the admin work. My dreams and ambitions were literally being fulfilled. I was a walking testament of a man who had everything materially. I didn't want to be king; I had no desire to be the Prime Minister; but the things that I had attained filled up my heart and my mind – nothing seemed to be lacking.

Routinely, as a member of the British Team I had to have regular medical check-ups. The check-up at this particular time yielded a surprise for me. The doctor discovered a growth in the back of my throat. I needed an operation straight away. If I continued to lift, it could cause the growth to burst. I didn't want to think about the repercussions of such an event. I thought about it for a moment. The problem was that I was supposed to be competing in the British Championships in two days – I had to be there to defend my title. I did go to the competition and I won it. The operation took place the next day and that too was successful. A fleeting thought passed through my mind, at this time: was I – a mere mortal – or someone who couldn't be touched by human weakness? The appearance of the growth, and the subsequent removal of it, had dented my armour. I shook the thought off, and bounced back to my normal way of seeing life.

The pressure of work built up. It required more time and effort and so my competing had to be put on hold. I had to apply myself to my work, as otherwise, it would have spiralled out of control; and if I wasn't taking care of it – who would?

The years sped by. Never did I stop training. I continued to push myself, even though I was not training for a championship. Training was my time for myself, and I thoroughly enjoyed it.

In 1985, I decided that it was time to start lifting again. I notified the British authorities that I wanted to compete again and they put me straight back on the team, without having to prove to them, my fitness and strength. My reputation preceded me. I was chosen to go and compete in Holland, but I was disappointed in my performance. I came third, when I had had high hopes of doing much better. My intention, as always, had been to win it.

This was the second dent in the self-made armour.

Chapter 2

COKE – THE REAL THING!

'He's gone' said Frank.

'What d'ya mean, he's gone? What me Dad's up and left? He can't have done, he's sixty-three. Does me Mum know where he is?' I was confused.

It was the early hours of Sunday 11 August 1985. My wife and I had only just come home from a fortieth birthday party. The phone had rung as soon as we came through the door. There was silence at the other end of the phone, and then Frank, my parents neighbour spoke again: 'Your old man's dead.'

My mind went blank. I mumbled something into the phone receiver, and replaced it. Walking as though in a trance, I told Jacqui what had happened. She was just putting James, our son, to bed. Emma was spending the weekend with our neighbours and their children in a caravan. Jacqui, although as shocked as I was, quickly got James dressed again, and we set off to see my Mum.

It wasn't long before we arrived at my parents' house. All the lights were on in the house. Jacqui took James upstairs to bed. My Mum was sitting in the front room, opposite my Dad, staring at him through unblinking eyes. Dad just looked as though he was asleep. His legs were crossed and his head was on his chest. He still had his glasses on. Tentatively, I walked towards him, and kissed his cheek. Picking up his cardigan, I draped it over his body. Tears were flowing down Mum's face. I sat next to her, putting my arm around her shoulders. There was nothing that I could say, or wanted to say. We sat close together for a while, linked by blood, and by our pain.

The doorbell rang. It was my eldest brother Eddie: his face was white. Eddie stood over Dad and asked, 'Is he dead?'

'Yeah, he is' I said, nodding.

'No, I mean, is he really dead?'

'Yeah.'

I knew what he meant. It looked as though, if we had prodded Dad, he would have woken up. It just didn't seem real that he was gone. The ambulance turned up soon after Eddie, followed by the rest of the family. Once Dad had been taken away, we all sat together making plans for his funeral.

Back at work the sense of losing Dad was strong. In the last few years of my Dad's life we had become very close. We were mates, as well as father and son. He had worked for many years as a security guard, for a firm of Stockbrokers, but had retired due to ill health. Dad then found that he had too much time on his hands, so he had come to work for me. All my workers knew Dad – he was the type of person, that once you knew him, you never forgot him. His loss was felt by all.

Death – is final. My own sense of mortality was heightened by the gap that was created by Dad dying. I had no power (and neither has anyone else on earth) to prevent someone's death. All the money that I possessed couldn't bring Dad back. Never before, in such depth, had I confronted the extinguishing of life. The truth was – I had unconsciously assumed that I was going to live forever. Once, when I lifted 66 stone, the power that surged through me, caused me to not only feel superhuman, but made me feel that I could never die.

Insidiously, the fear of dying began to come upon me. It was like a black cloak that slowly enveloped my mind. As the days turned into weeks and the weeks became months, I found myself swinging in and out of dark, morbid moods. At times, it was hard to shake them off. Sometimes, the periods of depression were so tangible that it was like having another person inside of me.

Taking steroids exacerbated the problem. I was first prescribed steroids for a hip injury. The rapid healing that took place through taking steroids made me realise how powerful they were. I noticed how quickly my body recuperated after a strenuous bout of training. I progressed from taking steroids in tablet form, to injecting them. Unfortunately, the steroids didn't help my state of mind; in fact they made my bad moods worse. The black periods of my life then seemed to be more prevalent. Amphetamines helped me a lot. My mood upon waking in the mornings told me what frame of mind I could be in for the rest of the day. I changed that by popping a few pills. After a while, even the Amphetamines, didn't help and I was introduced to cocaine. Coke was surely the 'real thing'. The buzz that I got from coke was instant. When I was 'down in the dumps', thinking about life and what it was all about – whether life was worth living, and everything negative, I would snort some coke, and 'bingo', I would be riding high, soaring through the skies of my mind, nothing and no-one could touch me.

Getting my supply of drugs had never been a problem. The crowd of lifters that I was involved with also dealt in drugs. The ready supply was endless. Huge quantities of drugs came across from the Continent, and through any other channel that the drugs could be smuggled into England. The finance that was needed, about £200 per week, to keep me in my drug lifestyle, was wearing hard on my business. I was still turning over a good profit, but with a house in Spain, and one in Loughton, plus my family to support, I needed to look for another avenue of income. I needed ready, hard cash.

Mickey (one of the guys that I was training with) and I, used to have a right laugh together. He was into a bit of gear. I knew that he didn't have a regular job, and I wondered how he managed to keep his life together. 'Door work, Arfer.' It didn't appeal to me. Standing outside some nightclub for five or six hours didn't seem like a good way to earn some dough. But the need for drugs surmounted any prejudice I had about being a bouncer. Within a short space of time, I found myself being a doorman for the Country Club, in Epping, Charlie Chan's in Walthamstow and Mr. T's in Erith, Kent. £50 to £100 a night gave me more money to snort coke. The glamour of the nightclub scene began to affect me too. The whole atmosphere: the music, the smell, the sights of everyone dressed up and reeking with aftershave or perfume, was heady stuff. I had never experienced this type of life before. It was new to me. I wanted more and more. It made me realise that up until that point in my life, I had been very naive to the ways of the world. Yes, I had transacted business deals. Yes, I had a wife and children to support. But, the darker side of life – wheeling and dealing, drugs, illicit sex – was new to me.

The highlight of any week would be to do a job at an illegal rave. These were mainly held in Barking, East London, usually on a Saturday night. More than eight thousand people would turn up at any one time to a rave. People would start coming from about 9 p.m. and they would dance and freak out to the music until seven the next morning. The reason that they were able to keep it up was because most of them were high on drugs. As doormen, it was our job to body-search everyone that came onto the premises. This netted us a good booty of drugs for ourselves. When the rave was over, we would divide the spoil! The pay for a night's work was the best I ever got – anywhere – about £300 to £400. All round, it was a fantastic night out.

Business was still good, but I was feeling restless. No longer did I feel like me. Since I had started to heavily indulge in drugs and had become a doorman, my mind and my lifestyle had become split into different compartments. Dr. Jekyll and Mr. Hyde didn't have a thing on me! At home I was the dutiful husband and father. It wasn't hard for me to maintain this role, as I still loved my wife and kids very much. But, once I donned my persona as a doorman, my personality underwent a change. Having the dinner jacket on my back, which was part of my uniform, the feeling would come over me that I was ready for any challenge that came my way. I could sense the violence within me building up: it hovered just under the surface of my emotions. I was able to control it – just about. Outside the nightclub doors, my eyes would scan every punter. Watching and waiting for something to go off. When it did, I was instantly ready. I would pounce like a tiger, seeking the core of the trouble, picking off the source, and overwhelming the person with my, now unleashed, violent strength. I never failed.

Keeping up appearances was beginning to wear me out. I wanted to remain a doorman – it was my regular business that I was concerned about.

1987 saw a lot of changes for me. I met a guy, Danny, during the course of my work as a doorman, who owned a large building company. We got talking. 'If ever you want some work, 'ere's my card, give me a call.' I toyed with his proposal. Maybe, this could be my way out. The responsibility of running my own business was getting on my nerves. Having to keep things ticking over was getting too much for me. The job offer looked more and more appealing. I called Danny about the job. 'It's all yours Arfer.' I didn't have to be told twice: I wound my business up, much to the annoyance of some of my men. But I was strictly thinking about me – I didn't care about them.

My new job, as a contracts manager, not only paid a good wage, but I got a company car too. The company was not only good to me, they even offered Jacqui a job in their offices. So in a way, we were still working together. With the pressure of running my own business off my back, I decided it would now be a good time for me to do some more competing.

Being a life member of the British Amateur Weightlifting Association (BAWLA), I was eligible to compete as long as I made the qualifying lifts which, being me, I was confident I could do. The 1987 British Championships were held in Milton Keynes. The last time I had been on a British platform, I had won. My confidence was high, I was sure that, once again, I was going to become a gold medallist. But my armour received another blow – I was beaten by Johnny Neighbour who wasn't in my class. In fact, he just wasn't on my level of achievement – yet, this man beat me – he blew me away. I was left reeling in shock at the outcome. Receiving the silver medal couldn't placate me.

Later in the year, I was picked to lift for Great Britain in the World Championships, in Norway. I gained second place, which I was happy with. The shadow of my loss at the British Championships was still like a cloud hanging over my head. My confidence had taken a whipping. Johnny Neighbour, through his win, had gone up a class and he went on to win the World Title.

My determination to win increased. Never again did I want to experience the negative emotions that I did, in losing out to Johnny. I trained harder: as far as I was concerned that was the answer. Looking around me, I noticed the effects of drug-taking in my fellow competitors. The drugs were becoming more scientific and sophisticated. The market was being flooded with the influx of drugs. Sources were unlimited, from the suppliers of the medical and the veterinary professions. The drugs that were used on horses and cows were coarser and had a greater impact on human beings. Whenever these drugs were available, everyone wanted them – they were in high demand. My supplier was excellent; he knew how to get hold of these drugs; it was just like purchasing confectionery. The more I consumed steroids, the more it seemed that amphetamines were no longer having much effect on me, so I stopped taking them.

My appetite for cocaine increased tenfold. I couldn't get enough of the stuff. It was very convenient that I worked the doors of nightclubs, because it made getting hold of coke that much easier. I was spending a couple of hundred quid a week fuelling my habit. Sometimes, depending on what was happening in my life at the time, I was spending even more. Coke became a way of life. People used coke as a form of currency. My reputation caused coke to fall into my life like snowflakes. People, it seemed, wanted to be seen with a celebrity – me. Lines of coke were constantly on offer, and I never refused.

The amazing thing was that my wife, Jacqui, never knew what I was up to. She was aware that I was using steroids because of an old injury, but had no idea how much I was taking. My personality changes, Jacqui put down to my work life. Having two jobs, she assumed, would stress anyone, plus I was training hard too. Her ignorance worked in my favour. Coke is a subtle evil. Insidiously, it crept upon me like smog, enveloping me, until I was completely immersed. I now needed coke to get through the day. My life was sweet.

I had had an on and off relationship with the Epping Forest Country Club. The club was very popular, in the Essex area, with a lot of young people. It was extremely fashionable, and the clientele would come from far and wide to dance the night away. I used to work the door, now and again, but, it wasn't until mid 1987 that I had a sort of permanent job there.

Donna was the receptionist at the Country Club when I first started working there: she was sixteen years my junior. We started off just having the occasional conversation: I was never more than a father-like figure to her. At five foot eight and a size ten, with legs that went on forever, I was sort of flattered that she wanted to talk with me. Her long blonde hair was dead straight, it always looked glossy and her face was always made up to perfection – she was beautiful. She was the sort of woman that, if I were younger and free, I would have made it my business to go after. Her personality was vivacious: she was always the life and soul of the party; she loved being the centre of attention. Donna was a flirt.

I don't quite know when my feelings for her changed, but they did. I used to drop her home from work now and again, and when

I pulled up outside her flat, she would peck me on the cheek, and say something like:

'I'd love to invite you in for a cup of coffee but,' looking me in the eye, she continued, 'you're a married man, and you need to go home to Jacqui'.

'Yeah, okay love, I'll be seeing you,' I'd reply. I would drive away pondering the situation between us. I mean, here she was, a young woman in the prime of her life. Would she really be interested in an old married man like me? Yet, the signals that Donna seemed to be sending out were ones of, 'Come and get me Arthur, I'm yours for the taking'. Were these thoughts a product of my imagination? Was the cocaine clogging my brain? Or was I just going mad? Whenever we were together, the atmosphere was charged with electricity: that was stimulating me, and I knew it was affecting Donna too. Or was it?

Chapter 3

COUNTRY CLUB AFFAIR

'The British Heavyweight Champion for 1988 – Arthur White.'

I had done it again. The accolade of the crowds, the hero-worshipping cries, boosted my drug-induced egotistic state of mind. I was flying high.

Mingling amongst the local crowd in Tottenham, I felt like Caesar. My friends and family were there, and their smiles and claps on the back caused my head and heart to swell.

'I'm so proud of you love' said Jacqui as she hugged me. She was always there for me, and it made me feel so good, knowing that she was pleased with me.

The months of training had paid off. As well as the steroid taking, the coke helped to put my mind in the right frame, and it enhanced the effect of the steroids: I felt marvellous.

The European Championships were a couple of months after the British Championships and they were being held in Germany. Again, I was more than confident that I was going to do well. The pressure was on, because I was competing against the World Champion, Ulf Morrin. He was a tough cookie, but I felt that it was something I could handle. I did it.

'The European Heavyweight Champion for 1988, from Great Britain – Arthur White.'

The national anthem was being blasted out as I stepped off the rostrum. The trophy was a huge affair, which I held above my head, to the cheers of the spectators. Friends of mine who had travelled all the way from England were ecstatic.

The European organisers knew how to put on a 'do'. There was a banquet with an abundance of food and drink. A live band played. It was a fantastic end to a fantastic day. I phoned home and told everyone that I had won, and that a grand slam was on the cards. British, European and the next for me would be the World Title.

In the mini-bus that was driving us back to our hotel, high in the mountains on the German/Austrian border, the weather suddenly changed. The light of the early evening was instantly swallowed up by a thick darkness. Looking out of the window, I saw the clouds turn black, and it started to thunder, with lightening flashing all around. It frightened me, but I never showed it to my colleagues. My heart thudded and I felt that something was wrong. But what?

At home, I settled back into normal life. I revelled in my new title, and people flocked to me wherever I was. Newspapers reported my win, and I even did a few television interviews. This was the life for me. I started to imagine what response I would get when I brought home the World Title trophy. Snorting coke helped keep my mind buzzing along those lines. Then, I received a letter:

'. . . you have been tested positive at the European Championships. The banned substance Neandrol was found in both of your urine samples. Therefore, your title has been stripped, and you have now been banned from competing for three years.'

I was gutted – but not too surprised. I was planning to contest their action, but the truth of the matter was, I was guilty. It would have been useless trying to proclaim my innocence when they had me over a barrel. All I could do was shrug my shoulders and carry on. I decided to join another organisation that weren't so stringent in their testing. They opened their arms and welcomed me into their company. They soon shipped me off to South Africa for their

World Championships.

I was happy: the weather was great; the people were hospitable; the food was marvellous; and I won. I was competing against a twenty-four-year-old, named Thor Kristy. He was shocked that I had beaten him to the post. He was a great 'bear' of a man, and it stunned him that a thirty-eight-year-old had knocked him back to second place. This was my first World Title.

The thirteen-and-a-half-hour flight from South Africa went by in a hazy blur. The booze was free, so, with two new friends I met on the flight, both professional golfers, we took advantage of the drinks trolley.

Walking through Heathrow airport I couldn't wait to meet Jacqui. As soon as my eyes saw her, my heart started to beat faster. Half running and half walking, I made my way to her. Throwing our arms around each other we hugged and kissed. 'Well done Arthur,' she said.

'Thanks darling, it's good to be home', I replied.

Jacqui drove home. Pulling up outside the house, I was amazed by the decorations that covered the house:

'WELL DONE ARTHUR – WORLD CHAMPION.'

The whole family had gathered to congratulate me. I was well chuffed. This had made winning the World Title all the more important for me. To be around my family was the best prize that I could have.

Once again, after such a momentous event, I bumped back down to earth. Normality took over as I went to work, and continued to do the things that were a part of my every day life. The following week I returned to work at the Country Club. There was a lot of back-slapping, and words of congratulation. The champagne, and the cocaine, was in abundance. All these things taken together caused my head to swell: life was like a party.

I gave Donna a lift home that night. She was full of praise for me and my achievements. We had a good chat as I drove the car. Then she dropped her bombshell. 'Eh Arf, I've got somethin' to tell you.'

'What's that love?'

Taking a deep breath she said, 'I've not been feeling too well recently, so I've decided to go back home to my Mum's in Wales'. Her words took me completely by surprise.

'Okay then love, keep in touch.' Donna climbed out of the car.

'Bye Arf.'

She didn't offer her phone number to me, and I didn't ask. I felt a bit crestfallen as I drove back home. I was a bit relieved that she was going away, as the temptation to have got involved with her was very strong. Now, I had escaped that. Yet, on the other hand, I would have liked to have got to know her better.

Within a few weeks Donna was gone. I left the Country Club soon after, myself, and started to work at another nightclub called Charlie Chan's, in Walthamstow. All round, it was a much better club for me to be working at. Some of the other doormen were my training partners. The money was way better than what I was getting at the Country Club, and the clientele were a bit older, and better behaved: which, all in all, made my working life easier.

One of the barmaids at Chan's was a friend of Donna. She came up to me and slipped a piece of paper into my hand and whispered: 'Donna said to give her a call'. As she walked off, I looked at the paper in my hand: it had a telephone number on it. I called her a few days later.

During the next few weeks I phoned Donna and we had some really good conversations: she sounded a lot brighter: almost like her old self. Then I was asked to be an official referee at a weightlifting competition in Cardiff, where Donna was living. When I told her, we made a date to meet up. I was excited that I would soon be seeing her. I couldn't wait for the competition to finish so that I could meet up with Donna. I had reserved a table for that evening, in the hotel where I was staying. Standing in the shower, I pondered what the outcome of the evening might be.

Never in my married life, up until this point, had I looked at another woman. Jacqui fulfilled me in every way and, therefore, there was no need for me to let my mind wander into such fanciful territory. But I have to say that since I had begun door work, the whole world of nightclubbing, drugs, sex and immoral behaviour had become more and more appealing to me. From an early age, I had known who I wanted to marry, and I did. The lifestyle that I was now experiencing was like watching television. I wanted a slice of the action.

The water washed away the soapsuds, as I nervously tried to reason with myself. I was a married man, and Donna was just a friend. I wasn't like other men, and I had vowed to be faithful to my wife. And yet . . .

The phone rang. Wrapping a towel around me, I answered it. Replacing the phone, my heart raced as I tried to get dressed hurriedly. Donna had turned up early, and was on her way up to my room. Buttoning my shirt quickly, I walked over to the door in response to the knocking. Donna looked radiant. My tongue cleaved to the roof of my mouth and I found it hard to talk to her. She didn't appear to have any problem being in my company.

'I've booked a table for us,' I said.

Looking me straight in the eye she replied: 'Un-book it. Let's just sit and talk'.

I did as she said and ordered room service and a couple of bottles of wine. By the end of the evening we were both feeling mellow. One thing lead to another.

The next morning I had mixed feelings: guilt was mingled with excitement. This was the first time that I had spent the night with any woman other than my wife; and a woman, who was a great deal younger than me. Cardiff and London were cities full of young, virile men, yet Donna had chosen me.

I had now begun a new 'other' life. Lying and deception became an integral part of my life and my coke habit increased tenfold. Donna was still living in Wales and I would phone her often during the week. In order to see her, I had to lay elaborate plans, and cover a lot of mileage. Cardiff was not just around the corner from where I lived in Loughton, Essex; yet, my desperation to see her drove me like a pack of wild dogs, every Friday, to Wales.

I had to increase my workload, to keep up with the expense of seeing Donna, but eventually, she decided to come back to London to live. I arranged a flat for her to live in, and a car. To make me look even better in Donna's eyes; I gave her money each week and paid all her debts off. I was the best thing that had happened to Donna. She told me about the men she had had relationships with in the past, and how most of them had treated her terribly. I was something different altogether.

My feelings of guilt towards Jacqui diminished, as my affair with Donna went on. Jacqui was completely in the dark about my 'other life'. Never did I withhold anything like money from her, or the children. The only thing that they didn't get much of was me. I spun Jacqui lies about needing to work longer hours, and about attending bogus competitions. She swallowed it all, hook, line, and sinker.

I was only able to see Donna in between my busy work and home life, but it just wasn't enough, for both of us. We made a plan. Donna had worked out that the only way we would be able to be together, forever, was if we ran off. I agreed. We both came up with the same destination – South Africa. You couldn't get any further away, as far as we were concerned. I was confident that Jacqui would never find out. I was careful not to be seen with Donna in public – we would only meet in the flat. Everything was going along in the right direction. Soon, I had planned, we would be sitting under the hot sun in South Africa. I had already worked out in my mind that on the day that we went, I would write a note for Jacqui telling her that I was off. But she found out sooner than I expected.

To enter South Africa you need to obtain a visa. I had the application forms in my briefcase. Jacqui had to look in my briefcase to get our chequebook out, and she spotted the forms. 'What are these?' She held the forms up in her hand. I made up an excuse and eventually, after many tears and arguments, she believed me. I think tearing up the applications in front of Jacqui, reassured her. I hugged and kissed her, knowing that this would comfort her. In my mind I was still trying to work out how I could get away. I later found out that I could apply for a visa when I got to South Africa. Even better!

My mind was definitely made up – I was leaving my wife and children. My heart had hardened to steel: there was nothing that could change my mind.

I had engineered a plan to sell our house. I wanted Jacqui in a smaller house, so that when I left, she would be able to keep up the expense of running it. We quickly sold it, and the guy who bought it paid us a large amount in cash. I banked it.

A week before we moved into the new house, I took off. I left Jacqui a 'Dear John' letter with £500. I withdrew £35,000 from our account and set off for a new life in South Africa. I hadn't told a soul that I was going to South Africa, so when Jacqui tried to find out where I was, she encountered a blank wall.

At first, South Africa was everything we expected it to be. We had money to burn. Our days were spent by the beach, and we danced and drank the nights away. Donna used drugs as well, so we would drop lines of coke day in and day out.

Then, when we were at a house party I met up with a woman who was an expatriate and, for some unknown reason, I related my situation to her.

'It sounds to me like you don't know what, or who, you want.'

Until that point in time, I hadn't thought too much about my wife and children, but the words that woman had spoken to me made me think.

Unbeknown to me, Donna had heard those words too. She had been in the next room. When I went to look for her, I couldn't find her: she had left the party, so I searched the streets for her. She was upset. In the car she told me what she had heard and asked, 'You haven't got over Jacqui, have you?'

'I have, but I miss the kids,' I replied.

There was still a part of me that really wanted my wife, but I couldn't say that to Donna.

I couldn't settle after that. A restlessness took over me. Each day that passed was one of torment. No longer was the sun and sand holding any attraction for me, and Donna no longer held the same deep attraction for me: I couldn't envisage spending the rest of my life with her. But, and it was the 'but' that caused my mind to revolve like an automatic door, there wasn't anyone that I could confide in. Slowly, my life was becoming like a hell in paradise. There was only one course of action open to me. I had to go home. Donna was quiet, while I packed the holdall full of my necessities: namely, drugs. I told an upset Donna, 'I'll be back'.

At London airport Jacqui didn't recognise me. I had lost weight, I looked drawn, and unshaven. For the last few weeks, sleep had eluded me. I had tried to blot out my troubled thoughts with alcohol, but that hadn't fully worked: I was in a state. Jacqui, being the wonderful woman that she is, welcomed me into her arms. It was as though I had just returned from one of my many weightlifting trips aboard. We stood like that, locked in each other's arms for a while, as the bustle of the airport swirled around us.

'Come on Arthur, let me take you home.'

I handed her my holdall: 'Get rid of that Jacq. What's in there has been the cause of all my troubles.'

Christmas was around the corner. I had chosen the right time to be at home, and my children had even forgiven me. I had promised Jacqui, with my hand on my heart, that I would never leave her – never. Jacqui's eyes spoke volumes to me. I could see that she really wanted to trust and believe me, but she just wasn't sure.

Within a couple of days, I had broken my promise. New Year's eve, 1989 saw me pack my bags and leave my wife – again. I had phoned Donna's mum in Wales. She had told me that Donna was due back home soon and I decided that I would meet her. What I had done to Donna was very wrong: leaving her in South Africa alone was an awful thing to have done. I worked out in my confused mind, that I should do the right thing and make it up to her.

The day I left for Wales was torment. I walked along the road towards the train station, with my holdall. Jacqui and the children were driving along at a snail's pace in the car, as they tearfully pleaded with me to stay with them. The scene tore at my heartstrings. But, not enough to convince me that staying would be good for them, or me.

My reunion with Donna was, at first, full of recriminations. After a couple of drinks and a meal she soon came round to my way of thinking. Throughout that time I spent with Donna, I felt that I wanted to spend the rest of my life with her and she believed me. Donna didn't want to live in Wales, and I certainly didn't, so I planned to get us a place nearer to home. I managed to rent a flat in Sawbridgeworth, and began another 'new life' with Donna.

Life is a funny thing. Sometimes you can have everything that your heart desires, and yet you're still not happy. Donna, who seemed perfect to me in every way, didn't do that much for me when we lived together and I soon realised, again, that we couldn't.

So, once again, I did my disappearing act. I left her.

Chapter 4

DEBT COLLECTOR

'There he goes. Watch that man he's evil.'

'He's working for Joe. Keep clear of 'im.'

'The guy's tooled up, he nearly killed Jimmy.'

I could hear the voices of the men, as I strolled through Spitalfields fruit and vegetable market in Bishopsgate, London. My trench coat flapped open as I looked from side to side at the different wholesale stands. I wanted to laugh. One fight, and now I was reputed to be as bad as one of the Krays.

The fight had taken place the night before, in The Gun pub, in Bishopsgate. My brother's friend Joe was a rich man, who owned a wholesale business in the market. His turnover was millions of pounds each year. He was having a problem with the market traders. He operated a credit system whereby you bought the goods, sold them, and then you paid what you owed. Unfortunately, some of the men were unscrupulous, and had no intention of paying Joe the money that they owed him. Jimmy fell into that category.

That evening, Joe was boozing away, whilst I was drinking Pepsi. I had taken some lines of coke, to keep me alert. Joe got into an argument with Jimmy, and Jimmy whacked him on the chin. Joe fell on the table, and landed on the floor. He was not a fighter, and I knew that if he didn't get any help, he would be done for. So I stepped in. Grabbing hold of Jimmy, I smacked him in the mouth. A full bottle of champagne was on the bar; I hit Jimmy across the face with it. As he staggered back, I hit him again. Jimmy didn't know what was happening to him, but I wasn't finished yet – I was only just warming up! I was well aware that I had to prove myself to Joe. The whole point of meeting him that evening had been to make an agreement about being his debt collector.

My speciality was to 'throat' somebody. Being a champion 'dead-lifter', my grip was like a vice: I would grab someone by the throat, which would quickly cut off their air supply, causing them to faint. Their arms would go limp, and just before they passed out, I would give them one powerful smack, which sorted them out good and proper. Jimmy experienced my technique. I dragged him through the bar doors, and continued to beat him. By now, he wasn't able to put up any resistance. I took his keys out of his pockets, opened up the door of his Mercedes car, and threw him onto the front seats. Blood was pouring out of him like a leaky kettle. I told him in no uncertain terms, that if he didn't pay Joe what he owed him, he would be getting more of the same, but in double doses. He paid up!

It was after 2 a.m. As I walked through Spitalfields, the tale of my exploits had already reached the market traders. Although the situation seemed comical to me, I knew that some of the punters that I would have to deal with wouldn't be easy pushovers, like Jimmy. I needed to get tooled up.

Joe was ecstatic with my performance. Now, he was confident that he would recuperate all that was owed to him, and he had his own personal bodyguard – me. Because Joe was pleased with me, he dutifully paid me £5,000, as a retainer. This money was a sort of down payment on any future worked I carried out on Joe's behalf. I felt good that, once again, I had some decent cash. The nature of the job was such that I knew that I had to kit myself out with some tools.

That very afternoon, I found a shop in Leyton, nearby where I was now renting a bedsit: it was a fishing accessories shop. I purchased a 12-inch Diver's knife. The shiny steel blade made me feel well able to deal with any punter that dared to challenge me. The knife case had two straps which, normally, divers would wear strapped to the outside of their leg. I fastened it to the inside of my forearm, with the handle pointing down to my wrist. It made access to the knife, in an emergency, easier. I got a list of names, from Joe, of the people that owed him money. My days were spent visiting various markets, collecting Joe's dosh.

I met up with one guy called Ted in the Camden Lock market. He was very reluctant to pay up and didn't like being threatened by the likes of me.

'Listen mate' he pointed his finger in my face, 'I know Lenny McClean, he'll sort you out.'

I knew of Lenny, and shrugging my shoulders I said to him, 'I'll see about that. I'll be back.'

Lenny McClean, was known in the East End of London as The Guv'nor. He was a prizefighter who could never be beaten. People were terrified of him, and one never used his name lightly, unless you were sure he was on your side. I had met up with Lenny some years previously when we were training together in a gym. I knew of his fighting skills, and he knew of my strength in power-lifting. We showed each other a fair bit of respect. I never doubted for one moment that he feared me, but I knew that I couldn't cross him.

So I used my 'loaf'.

Lenny was working at the Hippodrome nightclub, in Leicester Square, London. I went to the club to meet him. The big bouncers on the door didn't want to let me into the club initially.

'Who are you?' they asked.

'Don't worry about who I am: I've come to see Lenny. Tell him Arthur White wants to see him.'

Two of them walked off. Within minutes they returned and said 'Follow us'.

They led me to a dark little office at the end of a corridor. Lenny was as large as life, all $19^{1}/_{2}$ stone, in a dog's-tooth check jacket.

In a very gruff voice he said to me: 'Ello Son'.

I told him the story about the guy from Camden Lock market threatening me with Lenny's name and filled him in on Joe's story, and the money he was owed. He agreed to come and work with me – it was an easy way for him to earn a few quid. Turning to leave, Lenny said: 'That, will cost yer a monkey' (£500). I paid him there and then. Lenny was now on my firm, which meant I had a lot of power.

My reputation grew in leaps and bounds. Many people thought I was Lenny's younger brother: we looked quite alike. I never dispelled those rumours; it was good for business. We were very successful in our debt-collecting. When people saw us turn up, we aroused fear, which caused them to cough up the dough quickly. It was a lucrative business. Whatever we amassed for the day's work, we creamed off our percentage first, and gave Joe the rest. The following week, when I went back to see Ted, I told him Lenny was now on my firm and he paid up posthaste!

There was one guy called Johnny. He alone owed Joe a small fortune. Johnny was like a shadow – very elusive – he was hard to track down. I discovered where his office was and one day I broke into it, and smashed it up. I left a message with the guy in the office next to him: 'Tell Johnny that I'll be back'.

Early one morning, at Spitalfields, Johnny came to Joe's stand. He didn't see me at first, and I never gave him a chance to react. I pounced on him, like a cat after a mouse. I 'throated' him, and threw him against a palette-load of tomatoes – 144 boxes. He and the tomatoes went flying. I kicked the squashed boxes of tomatoes out of my path, to get a strong grip on Johnny again: I sorted him right out. Being a shrewd man, he settled a large part of his debt and skulked off, licking his wounds. Johnny knew that my debt-collecting was illegal and he turned up a few hours later with the police, who cautioned me. Johnny thought that once he had got the police onto me, I would back off. He didn't know me. I found out where he lived and then threatened to burn his garage down, along with his house. I was determined to win – to get him to pay up. Johnny knew I was getting too close for comfort and, eventually, he coughed up. It was a nice little earner for me.

Most of the time people paid up, but there were always one or two of them, who thought they were a bit clever, and could give me a knock-back. Billy was one of them. He was a wide-boy, who thought he was razor-sharp. He owned a number of fruit stalls, but, he was forever dodging Joe: he didn't want to pay up.

'Fancy a drive in the country Lenny', I asked one day.

'Alright boy', he answered.

We motored to Epping, where Billy had a large stall in the street market.

'. . . You have owed ten grand for a long time. It's pay up time. I want the first instalment – now', I threatened.

'But, I 'aven't got it. Look, see me next week and . . .'

'No, you look. I want two grand now, and we'll talk about the rest later.'

While I was busy negotiating terms and conditions, Lenny, who was standing beside me, was getting agitated. He had a lot of nervous energy building up inside him. He let out a bestial roar and, hooking his hands under the corner of the stall, he turned the lot over. The stall's contents flew through the air, spewing into the road, and over the pavement. Women started screaming. Traffic was halted, because oranges and apples, cabbages and potatoes were flying everywhere. Not wanting to be outdone by Lenny, I grabbed Billy by the throat and his leather belt, and turned him upside down. The contents of his pockets fell on the floor, and his money pouch emptied all over the ground.

'Put me down, put me down', he screamed.

I threw him on the floor.

'Don't hurt me, don't hurt me', he whined, as he gathered up the money which was scattered all over the street. He knew we weren't messing about. Laughing, I took the money, and calmly walked off, warning, 'I'll be back next week Billy, so be ready'.

Driving away, I saw in my rear-view mirror, the mess we had left behind.

'A good morning's work', I grinned at Lenny. 'Ere's your monkey mate.'

* * *

The orange-flavoured 'Jubbly' produced the desired effect. I thought that the triangular ice-pop would do the trick in numbing my neck, making it easier to cut – thus ending my life.

I had bought it that morning at about five o'clock from the corner shop. When I asked for it, the shopkeeper looked at me as though I was crazy. I suppose it was a strange thing for someone to request in December.

Driving through Homerton, east London, I knew it was the right time. I turned into a side road. The morning was dark and cold: it reflected how I was feeling inside. Tears ran down my face. For the last few days I hadn't slept and whenever my eyes became tired, I would lay on my bed, with a towel over them. My cocaine consumption had increased to a new high. All the money that I was earning was being snorted up my nose – I didn't care. My life was such, that cocaine was my only companion. The bedsit I was renting was bereft of life and warmth. I had to push all thoughts of my life at home with my wife and kids completely out of my mind. Even Donna wasn't very interested in me – she had turned her charms on to someone else. That's how much she cared for me!

Living no longer held any pleasure. Death was beckoning with powerful arms, waiting to engulf me. The familiar shroud of blackness, slowly, stealthily, crept over me. I welcomed it. Leaning my head back against the headrest, I tried to gain control of the battle that was raging in my heart and mind. My heart was crying out for help: help from someone – anyone – to stop me from doing what I had set out to do to myself; help from someone to sort my life out; help from someone, to just help me. Yet my mind was closing the lid on my life: it's too late; there is *no-one*; you're all alone mate. That's it. Finito. Finished. Done. Dead.

Audible sobs broke out from my lips.

'Oh Jacqui, what have I done.'

My mind jumped from the faces of my father, my mother, my siblings, my children, from people that I knew, to the people that I had given a hard time to. No-one was here for me now. The Jubbly had numbed my neck. I withdrew the diver's knife from its sheath.

The dawn was breaking – it was now or never. Lifting the blade up, I looked at myself in the rear-view mirror. Those eyes that reflected back weren't mine. The blackness in them seemed to have no end. Shutting my eyes tight, I gripped the handle of the knife and placed the blade against my cheek.

Time stood still.

For what seemed like an eternity, the blade slowly opened up the skin of my cheek, sliced through my neck, and down across my chest. Blood spurted out like a garden hose. With my eyes still shut, I sensed the warm stickiness of my blood, pumping out all over me. I wondered how long it would take for my heart to realise that my blood was no longer coursing around my body. I managed to replace the knife in its sheath. A heaviness weighed me down. This is it, I thought. My last few moments on earth. Fleetingly, I wondered where I was going, I hoped that it would bring the relief from this life that I desperately needed.

Dying was taking a bit of a time.

I started the car and drove deeper into the East End of London. My hope was that I would lose consciousness, and crash the car. That would definitely be the end of me. I thought about other people being involved in an accident, but the truth was, I didn't care. I just wanted out of this miserable existence.

Unfortunately, the blood that, half an hour ago, was being pumped out, had now dwindled to a halt. My clotting agents were working overtime. The cut on my cheek, to my disgust, was congealing. The realisation that I was going to live, caused me to break down in a torrent of tears and anguish. Could I do nothing right?

Turning the car around I headed back to my bleak bedsit. Stripping off my bloodied clothes, I felt despair.

From then on, everything became an effort, but, I forced myself to go to work. I didn't see any point in hanging around my flat. Maybe, I could earn enough to buy a big stash of gear, and blow my brains out. Walking through Spitalfields, I noticed that people were looking at me on the sly. Nobody questioned me about the cut on my face and I let them reach their own conclusions. They probably assumed that I had been in a violent fight. They would have been right, in a way – the fight being with myself!

* * *

The hot sun was beating down on my skin with a vengeance. I was tanked up with coke and cheap wine. Tenerife.

Donna and I had decided at the last minute, to hop on a plane, and see some of the world. The fact that for nearly two weeks we had hardly communicated with each other didn't disturb me too much. We had gone through the motions of trying to resurrect our relationship, but I knew it was dead. Still, I tried to enjoy myself, regardless. My mood, even on holiday, was a yo-yo of confusion. One minute, I would be flying high, the next, I would plunge into the depths of depression.

Early one morning, I took myself off to the beach, alone. I had just called Jacqui at home, and told her a pack of lies.

'I'm here on business love.'

'On business, in Tenerife. Don't take me for a fool Arthur.'

'No, no, straight up Jacqui, I'm collecting money.'

'Okay, okay', she sighed.

Replacing the handset, I knew she didn't believe me, yet, I had a weird compulsion to hear her voice. Now, she was even more suspicious of me. I shouldn't have bothered.

Sitting on the beach, I watched the sun, grow brighter and brighter, as the day broke forth in all its brilliance. It was difficult for me to think clearly. This was paradise – but, here was I, my mind in sheer hell and torment. The waves were gently lapping to and fro. What should have put me in a tranquil mood, stirred up giant feelings of guilt, remorse, anger, sadness and loneliness, to name but a few. The motion of the waves was enticing. It was so tempting to just stand up and walk towards their beckoning call. Taking deep breaths, I was just about to walk off into a watery grave, when a voice said:

'You cannot take your own life.'

There was no-one around. It was natural for me to address the voice, looking up into the cloudless sky.

'Who are you?'

Anyone walking by would have assumed that I was a regular fruitcake, and given me a wide berth, when they heard me talking to myself.

The voice answered: *'I am your Father'*.

Snorting, I replied, 'You're not my Dad, my Dad's dead'.

Peering up into the sky, I waited for an answer. I thought I had glimpsed a face among the clouds, but I couldn't be sure. Shaking my head, I suddenly realised that I had finally flipped my lid.

'I'm going crazy' I said to no-one. 'I'm having a conversation with myself.'

I forgot about topping myself. Instead, I went back to the hotel and did a few lines of coke to block everything out.

The holiday was soon over. Stansted airport is small in comparison to the other two main London airports. Walking through customs, Donna and I probably looked like all the other sun-baked, relaxed, holidaymakers. In reality that was far from the truth. I didn't notice that among the relatives and friends that were in the arrivals hall, waiting to meet their loved ones, was Jacqui.

I called her later to tell her that I was home. Lying through my teeth, I stuck to my story about being on a business trip.

'I saw you both.'

Those words were like a sharp knife piercing me, right down to the bone. I would have continued to lie, but Jacqui had caught me out. I slammed down the phone.

After a couple of weeks in the sun, nothing had been resolved. Increasingly, death looked like the way out. It was either that, or killing someone else and losing my liberty.

Chapter 5

FRESH START

'Arthur, stop!'

I was bent over my victim, pinning him to the tarmac with my knee. My left hand was wrapped around his head, as he lay immobilised on his left side. In my right hand I held my knife. Murder was not in my mind, but, teaching him a lesson was. I began to saw behind his ear lobe. My intention was to cut off his ear.

The guy that was soon to become 'earless' was a stranger to me. It was through Donna that this guy was now at my mercy. My relationship with Donna was in decline. We had barely been seeing each other. Even our telephone conversations were a thing of the past. The only reason I missed Donna was because, at the time, I was a lonely man. I would have been happy if a smelly, old tramp had come and kept me company. I really did miss my wife, though. It was painful to say her name, let alone think about it: that would have been torture. The flat at Leyton was never truly home to me. It was somewhere for me to rest my aching body, wash, and change my clothing.

One night I was having forty winks, when the buzzer for the front door sounded.

'Arfer, it's me Donna, I need to see you.'

'Alright, I'll let you in.'

The tone in her voice let me know that something was very

wrong. How right I was.

Tearfully she recounted to me the events that led her to seek me out.

'. . . Please Arfer, please could you sort him out? No way do I want him to get away with it. He needs to be taught a lesson.'

The gist of her problem was that she had had an altercation with a guy. It was drug-related. Her main concern was that she had come off worse: she couldn't live with that. That's why she had turned to me for help.

I was dressed in my jogging bottoms, with a singlet. The diver's knife was strapped to my arm, as normal, on view for all the world to see! The cold February night air chilled my exposed skin. I shook myself, and made my way to my car. Donna was up ahead, leading the way back to the nightclub in north London where her troubles had started. I parked my car in Tottenham High Road and we walked round the corner to the club. It was now about 1 a.m. The club's doors opened, and people spilt out like sewage.

In full view of the club punters, I stood with legs apart, arms by my side, and fists balled, ready for action. Rambo had nothing on me. Donna was standing just behind me. A man appeared at the door amidst a crowd of people.

'That's 'im', Shouted Donna.

The crowd froze. Then the guy who had had the run-in with Donna, must have recognised her. He broke free from his mates, and legged it. I was in hot pursuit. I hadn't taken any gear recently, but it was still in my system from the last hit. This guy was not going to get away. Adrenaline was pulsing through my body. For that moment in time, its effect was better than cocaine. I was buzzing.

The club was situated at the top of a 'dead end' street. At the far end of the street was a wall. The guy that I was pursuing hadn't done himself any favours by running down that street. There was no escape – he was trapped. He ran around a parked van. I had to stop him, so I grabbed the roof rack with one hand, and vaulted over the top of the van, landing in front of him. The guy turned to flee. I stabbed him once in the back. He continued to run, so I stabbed him again. He stumbled, and fell. I pounced on him, like a tiger. In shock, the guy feebly tried to resist me. I was in my element. To keep him still I gave him a couple of punches to his body, and his head. That stopped him. His right ear stood out to me, like a flashing neon light. That's when the idea of cutting it off, came to me. I would have completed the job, had it not been for the body-less voice.

'Arthur stop.'

I froze.

Looking around me, I was a bit spooked. There was no-one there. Yet, I had clearly, audibly, heard someone call my name.

The voice had broken my concentration. Not bothering to complete the job, I put my knife back into its sheath, and stood up. As I turned round, I was shocked to the core. Silently, in front of me was a crowd of about two hundred people. Whilst I had been busy, doing a butcher's job on the guy, the night revellers had congregated in a mass behind me. I knew that somewhere among the crowd, would be my victim's mates. I shrugged back my shoulders. Knowing that this guy had friends in the mob ahead, I guessed that I was in for a hiding. Being kicked about is no fun and I was worried that someone might have a knife.

I squared my jaw, and began to walk slowly towards them. I was preparing myself for a fight. No way was I going to go down begging for mercy. I would take it as it came and give as good as I got. Strength seemed to come from the air, as I continued to walk forward. I tried to catch people's eyes, as the distance between us shortened. At the edge of the crowd, just as I was bracing myself for the first blow, something strange happened. The crowd parted and formed two sides, with a path down the middle. I hesitated. Was this a trick? Would I get half way, only for them to close ranks – and that's the last of me? But no. As I walked through, the crowd continued to part, until I reached the other side and safety.

My car was still in the same place. Revving the engine, it suddenly dawned on me that Donna had disappeared. I didn't worry about that for long. What was the point? Within a short time, I was home, dressed and off to work. I put the whole incident out of my mind.

My drug habit was costing me, an arm and a leg. As soon as I earned a few quid, it would slip through my fingers, and down my throat, or up my nose. The flat was proving too expensive to keep on, so, I decided to give it up. But where could I go? Jacqui didn't want me at home anymore. At that point, I had left her and the children six times. She wasn't keen to take me back again and I didn't blame her. Donna, had turned into a right fly-by-night, and to be honest, the level of trust between us was zilch, so to stay with her wasn't an option either.

The only home in which I would be welcomed with open arms, was my Mum's.

'No problem son, anytime.'

I wondered what my mother would have thought if she had had an inkling of what I was up to. My mother was of a different era, and the drug culture was far removed from her way of life. She would have had a fit if she had known what was taking place under her roof.

The depressive, suicidal, mood that I had drifted into, was permanently a part of my sad life. There just didn't seem any point to anything. I took as much cocaine as I could get into my body. But, I had noticed that it wasn't having the same mind-blowing effects that it used too. So, I took more and more to achieve that high.

About four o'clock one morning, after leaving work, I had snorted some coke to pep myself up for some debt collecting. I was working alone now, which wasn't a bad way to work: though, if I needed to call on Lenny, I could. Cruising along Eastway in Leyton, a car behind me tooted and flashed. Initially, I ignored the driver, but he did it a second time. Anger sprang up like a volcano erupting. I pulled over to let him overtake me. Then, I 'gunned' the engine and tore after him. He began to drive more quickly. I flashed and tooted him. He kept looking at me in his rear view mirror: I could sense his fear. He wanted to get far, far away from me. I wanted to pulverise him. He drove his car into a cul-de-sac. Without parking his car, or turning the engine off, the guy leapt out of his car like Batman and took off. He disappeared into a block of flats. I walked up to his car, and shut the engine down. Taking his car keys out, I flung them down the nearest drain hole.

I scanned the dark flats for any sign of life – nothing.

'C'mon show yer face. C'mon let's see how brave yer are now?' I screamed at the top of my voice.

No response.

My anger over-spilled into the night air, as I filled the emptiness with profane expletives. I had psyched myself up for a good fight. Now, I could only plug up the hole with more drugs.

I was trying to make amends with Jacqui. I had come to terms with the fact that my relationship with Donna was past history. I would romanticise to myself, that a younger woman had an interest in me and everything was hunky-dory. But, it wasn't true: I didn't want her any more. In an ideal world, Jacqui and I and the children, would be reconciled and living together as one big happy family.

Real life had me still kipping at my Mum's. My mother wasn't happy with my situation, but there wasn't a lot she could do. I know that she was hoping that Jacqui and I would get back together, if only, for the children's sake. My Mum had old-fashioned views about family life. Jacqui and I, by now, were on speaking terms. Maybe, just maybe, she might forgive me, and take me back. I didn't want to push her too far, too soon. So, I kept my feelings under wraps.

One Saturday morning in February all of my nice family thoughts went into oblivion. Donna would periodically call me at my Mum's. We didn't have much to say to each other: it was more a case of passing the time of day. Unfortunately, this time Jacqui had chosen to pop in and see me, and she overheard my conversation with Donna. It wasn't the content that troubled her; it was the fact that Donna and I were still in contact with each other. As soon as I put the phone down, Jacqui erupted. It wasn't long before we were shouting and screaming at each other. The air was thick with my lies and deception and Jacqui was hurt.

'That's it. Never again. We are FINISHED.'

She stormed out of the front door without a backward glance. It was then that it really hit me that I was alone. I suppose I should have thought about how badly I had treated Jacqui. But selfishly, I was only thinking about myself. I knew then, in my heart of hearts, that this was the end of the long and turbulent road with my wife.

'No man is an island', so the saying goes, but I felt adrift from the rest of the human race. That night I went out and got hammered. I consumed so much coke and alcohol, that it was amazing that I remained standing. From that point on, I went on a bender. I would try to consume as much as I could. I really wanted to kill myself, but the next best thing, as far as I was concerned was to be so out-of-it, that I was only half aware of the real world.

I decided to meet up with a friend one night over the other side of the river Thames. We drank ourselves under the table, and afterwards I bid him goodnight, and set off, in a terrible state, for home. Blackheath was a distance from where my Mum lived. Driving along the lonely road, I noticed a road sign for Crystal Palace. I was going the wrong way. I spun the car around in one manoeuvre, and headed back the way I had come.

I have no idea what happened after that – I had a complete blackout.

A cold breeze ruffled my thin silk shirt. Stirring from my 'bed', I sat up. Even in my muddled state of mind, I could see that I had fallen asleep out in the open. To be more precise, I had taken refuge on a bench on Tower Bridge. The water swished beneath me. The early birds were flying up above me. How did I get there?

Dazed I looked around me. Where was my car? My tongue was like sandpaper, and my head was spinning. Staggering to my feet, I wasn't sure in which direction I should head. My feet seemed to know where they were going, so I followed them.

I ended up on Westminster Bridge. The thirty-minute walk woke me up. My car was parked on the bridge, with the keys still in the ignition. I climbed in and drove home. The whole event was worrying.

Up until now, I had been able to handle whatever had happened to me. Having blackouts was another thing altogether. Where had that time gone? I realised that I needed help, and I needed it now.

*   *   *

In 1990, Emma had joined a youth group at Epping Forest Community Church, when she was thirteen years old. She had been invited by a school friend. As the months went by, Emma became a Christian and later that year was baptised. She encouraged my wife and my son James that it would be the best thing for them too! Neither Jacqui nor I had ever had the inclination to go to church. It had never dawned on us that we should go to church, or even send our children. Christian living was not something that we had thought about much. Although, if anyone had asked whether we were Christians or not, the answer would have been 'yes'. (That was before I went off the rails!) We, along with many others, thought that being born in England, automatically gave us the right to label ourselves 'Christian': after all, this is a Christian country! I didn't know much about this Christian business. In fact I didn't want to know. Christianity was for wimps, I thought. What good was it for a 17-stone heavyweight, World Champion power-lifter?

Vincent Wiffin was an elder of the church that my daughter Emma attended. Jacqui had recommended him to me. It was Jacqui who told me what I already knew – that I was in desperate need of professional help. I felt I had no option but to contact this Vincent guy.

When I first met Vin, in 1993, I was a bit taken aback. Here, clearly, was no wimp. I was expecting him to be a bearded, longhaired, pebbly-spectacled, sandal-wearing freak. Vin was none of those. Meeting up with Vincent changed my life. It sounds a bit of a cliché, but for me it is absolutely true. Vin was no fool. He was a big guy, and could clearly handle himself. I had strapped my knife to my leg, as I usually did. I didn't figure he would be too much trouble for me, but I wasn't taking any chances. He knew more about me, than I did about him. That was a disadvantage in my book, but I kept cool and listened to what he had to say to me.

Quickly, we built up a rapport. He didn't preach to me, or bash me over the head with his Bible, or shout out 'Sinner, sinner get thee hence', which I was half expecting. It would have given me a good excuse to get up and walk out.

I was a first for Vin. He confessed that he had never met anyone quite like me before, and had been somewhat apprehensive about meeting me. His background was very different from mine. Living in a sleepy, middle-class village in Essex, he had not been exposed to the likes of me, and my lifestyle. Relating my life up until that point to Vin, helped me to put my thoughts into perspective. I think it opened up a whole new world for him too! Standing on his doorstep saying our goodbyes, Vin said a few words to me that have remained with me all my life. He said, 'Arthur, you have to choose'. As I walked away, his words gutted me more than anything else Vin had said to me at that meeting. I had to choose between Jacqui and Donna? I had to choose between my two beautiful children, or starting another family? Ultimately, I had to choose between good and evil. I had gone from a good life, with my family and job, and peace of mind to a life full of evil, drugs, violence, and an immoral relationship. At this place in my life, there was no peace of mind or heart. As for love: the capacity to love others, to receive their love, and to love myself had gone from me. I was full of contempt for myself. Looking at others, I could see my own problems reflected in people's faces: many people were selfish and so consumed with themselves, that they didn't even realise that love was missing from their lives. That is a sad, sad place to be at. I had thought I had reached rock bottom before, but this time it was different: I felt that I was on the road of no return.

It was a cold March morning, when, in Spitalfields market car park, I stood, looking up at the sky, with my arms outstretched and called out, 'Help me God'. I didn't know if that was how one prayed, but it was the best I could do, in my desperation. Arrogantly I asked God to come into my life and sort it out.

'God,' I continued, 'if you're so clever, you come and sort it out.'

There were no angels' wings flapping, no trumpets blowing, the sky didn't open up and belch forth any weird and wonderful manifestations. Absolutely nothing. And yet, a strange feeling enveloped me, soothing me, and I felt at peace with myself.

I wasted no time, in making a new start. I unstrapped my precious diver's knife, and threw it into a skip nearby. Back home at my Mum's I took a drastic step in emptying my cache of drugs onto the kitchen table. My Mum gasped in horror at the sight, taking in the fact that her darling youngest son was a drug addict.

I felt the need to share with people the new path that I had now chosen for my life. Vin was over the moon and congratulated me. He took me under his wing, and showed me that following Jesus Christ, was the only answer for my life, and that I would never again sink to those depths of depravity, as long as I stuck close by Jesus.

I met with Vin over the weeks that followed, for marriage guidance counselling, then for Bible study and prayer. As I continued to meet with him, my feelings of self-worth increased.

Vin was instrumental in getting Jacqui and I back together

again. Although Jacqui wasn't a Christian yet, she was well-known in the church, and some of the members were apprehensive about us getting back together too quickly. They were worried that I could be using God as an excuse, to get back with Jacqui. She wasn't convinced that I could change so quickly anyway.

The going was very slow and I missed my family desperately. I had a picture of them on my bedside, which I would sometimes hold tightly, sobbing my heart out, wanting so much to be back with them. The pain was awful. Jesus had now given me a new ability to love, and because I wasn't able to fully put it to use, it was causing an aching and emptiness. Out of the depth of my heartache for Jacqui and the children, I cried out to God:

'Lord, if it's not your will for us to be together, I'll accept it. But, I will never go back to the life I once lived, and turn away from you.'

I knew I had to pray that prayer: I wanted Jesus to know that I was truly His, and His alone, but I still desperately wanted my family back.

A few days later, Jacqui called me. It was 9.30 in the evening.

'Arthur, would you like to come over for a chat.'

As soon as I had put the phone down, I was up the stairs, two at a time. I showered and shaved, and splashed on aftershave in what must have been record time.

We sat and talked until about three o'clock in the morning. Jacqui wanted to take things slowly, to see whether there was any truth in what I was telling her. Time would tell!

As I stood at the front door, I asked her if she still loved me.

'I have always loved you Arthur. It's just that I can't trust you. I need to be sure.'

My hopes shot up a couple of notches. I believed then, that God was doing something in my wife. I was hoping that soon we would be together again. However, before my hopes of Jacqui and I being together again came to fruition, I had to square things with my children. This was a painful time for me. Again, it made me realise that my selfish lifestyle had caused a great deal of hurt to many people. My fear was that my children would reject me. What would I do then?

I sat them down one afternoon and told them about my life for the past seven years. It didn't sound good even to my ears.

'Kids, I have got to tell you both that your Dad was a drug addict.' A lump formed in my throat making it hard for me to speak. As I recounted my sorry excuse for a life, tears flowed like a river, cascading down my face and falling into my lap, my two lovely children, unspoiled by the world, cried along with me. The loss of our beautiful house, and the one in Spain, not to mention the fact that I let about £150,000 slip through my fingers or, more precisely, snorted up my nose. I had even stooped so low as to sell my wedding ring. At that time of debauched living, nothing had been precious to me. Everything was expendable.

My children were wonderful.

'Dad,' my children said to me, 'we're more proud of you now, than of anything that you have ever done in the past.' I couldn't believe that they were so forgiving. The fact that my children had not turned their backs on me, encouraged me to think that perhaps Jesus Christ wouldn't either?

* * *

Looking back on life, I have come across thousands of people, from all walks of life. Many will argue against the truth – about the existence of Jesus Christ, the Son of God. But, no-one can argue against the truth of my life. In the past seven years, since 1993, on that March morning, when I surrendered my life to Jesus, my life has changed completely. I'm free from my eight-year cocaine addiction; my marriage has been restored; I have the love and respect of my children again; I have a decent job; I have a lovely home; my health is fully restored. And to top all that, I

competed in and won another British and European title in the
same organisation, against the same competitors – and I was drug
free. On the arm of my tee-shirt was printed: 'The joy of the
LORD is my strength'(Nehemiah 8 verse 10).

I often say and believe, that I'm more of a man now, than I ever
was before. It takes a 'real man' to be a follower of Jesus Christ
in this dark, dark world. To claim that, in becoming a Christian,
all your troubles vanish, you get piles of money, and everything
turns out great, would be a lie. The truth is, that no matter what
your circumstances are, the joy of the Lord will be your strength,
and Jesus will help you through them.

JACQUI'S STORY

I love my husband – I always have.

Arthur was the sort of man that a woman would be proud to call
her own. He was a wonderful father and provider. Yet, in 1989, he
changed radically, and this change deeply affected my life.

Reading Arthur's story, may cause you to wonder, 'Well, what
about his wife?' She was mad to put up with him. She should have
got rid of him. She would have been better off without him.

When he first walked out on me, it was a complete hammer
blow to my heart. Emotions raged within me, tearing me apart.
Anger was like a bomb that would blow up again and again. Sadness would wash over me like a tidal wave, in which the sense of
drowning was overwhelming.

Throughout the four-year passage of time when Arthur was
involved with Donna, I knew that I had to hold myself together, not
only for the children's sake, but for my own sanity. Initially, I wanted
my Arthur back. But unfortunately, these are the days of a 'disposable
society', and as time went on I thought, 'Yeah, I'll forget about him,
and find someone else': but I thank God that that didn't happen.

I went from having a close, stable relationship with Arthur, to no husband, no money, and no father for my children – nothing. I didn't want to be another statistic, a one-parent family, but I had lost control of my life, through no fault of my own. The constant make-ups and break-ups took their toll on the children and I. I had always been a strong-willed woman – I don't get fazed easily – but the break-up of my family proved too much for me. I had been deceived and betrayed too many times by my husband. Friends helped me the best way they knew how. Michelle was a very good friend, who was more than a shoulder to cry on. My Mother was also a tower of strength. It was she who pointed out to me that this wasn't the Arthur we knew – something must be wrong. She was absolutely right. I was tired. I had reached the point of defeat and there was no more fight left in me. Then, Jesus Christ stepped in.

The work that Jesus accomplished on the cross was paramount in my reconciliation with Arthur. Jesus, who knew no sin, died because of my sin. The time came when I had to make a choice whether to forgive my husband – and put aside the things that he had done, that had caused so much hurt and pain – or not. There was no way I could forgive him in my own strength. Jesus Christ gave me a forgiving heart – his heart. That's how I was able to do it. But more than this, I had to choose Jesus above all else. If I had chosen not to forgive, Arthur and I would have remained apart forever. Forgiveness meant that we would have a chance to be a whole family again, but even if we didn't get back together, I still wanted to have a heart and mind free of bitterness and resentment.

I know that other women have been through the same, if not much more than I have. My words to them would be: 'The Lord is my light and my salvation: whom shall I fear? The Lord is the strength of my life: of whom shall I be afraid?' (Psalm 27 verse 1)

Someone asked my son James, if he had ever seen a miracle? He replied 'Yes, our family'. Thank you Jesus.

STEVE JOHNSON

Chapter 1

THIRST DRINK!

'Yeah mate, yer look alright.' I was admiring myself in the hallway mirror. The black stay-press trousers, and the sky blue Brutus shirt that I was wearing complimented my six foot two height. The horn of the mini cab sounded and I was out of the front door, and walking down the path in a couple of seconds.

I felt good. I patted my trouser pocket just to make sure that the wad of money was still there. I was looking forward to my evening out, drinking with my pals. The cab driver made small-talk about the hot weather. I just murmured a bit, here and there. I mean, what could you say about the weather being hot, after all, it was mid August! Anyway, my mind was on the evening ahead.

The car stopped outside The Retreat pub, and I paid the driver and got out. Straightening myself up, I brushed my trousers down, and looked around me. The pub was on the main road, the A13, right outside Ford's Dagenham production plant. I had worked as a contractor now and again, for Ford, and I was familiar with the set-up. The pub wasn't my regular now, but it had been in the past. I was known by the owner, and by many of the punters.

Pushing the door open, I was greeted by thick blue smoke. It was hot and sticky. The juke-box was belting out some heavy metal, head-banging sounds, that had me nodding my head in time to the beat, as I made my way towards the bar.

I had arranged to meet my mate Kevin at 6 p.m. It was now ten minutes past.

The Retreat was a real dive. The wallpaper was peeling off, and was an indescribable colour. It might have been pink, or yellow originally, but now, there was no way of telling. The paintwork was chipped and definitely in need of a couple of fresh coats. On the floor were quarry tiles that were ugly and stained. 'Retreat', was the wrong name – 'Bedlam' would have been more appropriate. Still, the poor decor didn't worry me, as long as I could get a drink when I wanted, that was fine.

'Steve.'

I looked over my shoulder and saw Kevin coming towards me, from the corner. He brought me a beer.

'Hello son.' He looked me over and said, 'I haven't forgotten we're going out'.

I was a bit put out that he hadn't changed his clothes: he was still in his work gear. But, what could I do?

'Look mate,' continued Kevin, 'I'll be with yer in a minute, I've just got to sort somethin' out.'

That didn't make me feel any better. I wanted to be on my way, not hanging around a dirty pub, waiting for him to get himself together. Reluctantly I picked up my pint and nodded at him as he walked back to the group of men that he had been with, when I came into the pub. I watched the blokes that Kevin was talking too. I had never seen them before, but I could sense that something bad was going down. Taking a few sips of my beer, I glanced over the rim of the glass at Kevin. The conversation he was involved in was getting heated. Scanning the pub, I noticed that Kevin's so-called pals, were not with him. It was as though they were turning a blind eye to his plight.

Kevin and I go back to 'pram-days': we lived opposite one another when we were growing up. He was like a brother to me. I cautiously walked towards him, all the time checking out the guys that were around him.

'Yer alright Kev?'

He nodded at me, but was still talking to a mountain of a man who stood bang in front of him. It was obvious to me that Kevin was under some sort of stress, so I repeated myself again. He didn't reply straight away, but the guy did.

'Does he look alright?' he sneered.

The two big black guys behind him laughed. Within a split second, I smashed the pint beer glass I was holding, into his face. The full force of my might, caused the glass to break against his teeth, and tear into his cheek. The blood spurted out like a fountain. He toppled over and fell to the floor, and landed on his hands and knees, where he spewed up his lunch! Panic broke out. The guy was squealing like a pig. The barmaids, who were the only women in the pub, screamed like sirens, and ran across to the guy. The atmosphere in the pub changed. Still holding the remainder of the broken glass in my hand, I said to the guy's two sidekicks: 'Do yer fancy some of this?' One of the guys dropped to his knees to assist his pal, and the other, an 18-stone body builder, backed off. I took two steps back, and with a slight run, I gave the guy on the floor a well aimed kick between the legs. He let out a bellow that I thought was going to bring the roof down.

Kevin realising that this meant trouble, quickly pulled me to one side and said, 'Disappear'. I shrugged, and then swore. Casually, I picked up a half-full pint glass and began to greedily drink the contents. I stood looking at the guy on the floor, covered in blood, with the bar staff trying to stem his blood loss with bar towels.

'Disappear, quick mate,' said Kevin apprehensively.

Something clicked in my brain at Kevin's concern. 'Okay, phone me,' I replied and calmly walked towards the door, and out of the pub. As I crossed the A13, I was feeling a bit upset, that the guy had spoiled my evening. What was supposed to be a nice night out, was now ruined – all because of him!

I walked down a few roads until I came to a small cab office that I sometimes frequented.

'Got a cab love?' I asked the girl in the office.

'There's one outside mate, local is it?'

'Yeah.'

As I turned to leave she said to me, 'Had an accident?'

Looking back, I asked her why.

'There's blood all over your hand.'

Holding my hand up, I could see that my thumb was deeply cut, and a piece of glass was in it. 'So there is.'

'Hold on, have some of these.' The woman handed me some tissues, which I used to wrap my thumb in.

The drive home was uneventful. I made the driver drop me off at the end of my road. I was being a bit cautious, as I didn't think it was wise to let him know where I was going, in case of any comeback.

I hadn't been in the house more than fifteen minutes, when the phone rang.

'Steve?' It was Kevin.

'The ambulance has just taken him away.'

'Is that right. So he's still alive then?'

We both laughed.

'Yeah. He's a geezer who's been taking liberties with the firm for the past three weeks.'

Kevin was the manager for a firm of contractors that was based at Ford's Motor Company, and the guy was a sub-contractor who Kevin had hired during the summer break. The guy thought that he was some sort of Mafia figure, and had been muscling in on the workers, demanding money, and taking liberties all around.

'Well Kev,' I said, still laughing, 'he won't be taking any now.'

That really made Kevin guffaw.

'Tell yer what Kev, I'll see yer up Spooners bar in half an hour.'

'Alright mate,' he agreed.

As I put the phone down, I realised that the tissue was now saturated with my blood. Upstairs in the bathroom, I couldn't find any plasters, so I used the next best thing – Sellotape. I pulled the piece of glass out and tightly wrapped my thumb with the Sellotape. The flow of blood slowed down. I thought that I would need to change my clothes, as I expected them to be covered in blood, but amazingly, not so much as a spot of blood was on them. I was clean: unstained by the past hour's events. The throbbing pain in my thumb was increasing. But I was determined to go out and have a good time. So, I ignored it.

As I walked down the road, I was feeling somewhat irritated that part of the evening had been wasted, when it could have been put to better use – drinking for example. I was pleased, though, that I had put a stop to someone who had been messing my mate about. Kevin had told me that the 'Old Bill' had turned up in the pub. Nobody had admitted to seeing a thing – I was relieved about that. The man would now be scarred for life. I hoped that every time he looked in the mirror, he would remember me.

I spent two days in agonising pain, before I eventually went to seek medical help for my thumb. I had been reluctant to go to casualty, in case I turned up at the same hospital as the guy who I had done over, and was linked to his 'accident'. Next thing I'd have known, the Old Bill would be picking me up, just as the last stitch was being sewn. Being devious, I went to a hospital far away from home, and gave them a false name and address, in order to get my thumb sorted out.

Years later I was to remember the guy whose face I had altered, because the same thing happened to me.

* * *

Dagenham, Dagenham. Can anything good come out of Dagenham?

Dagenham is a borough in east London. I loved living there as a child. At that time, in the 1960s and 70s, it was home to the biggest housing estate in Europe. Hundreds and hundreds of kids, had a similar upbringing. Families were large, money was short, but there was always plenty of dosh for booze. My family was a typical, working-class Dagenham family.

My dad was well-known locally – not because he was a millionaire, or a famous actor, or some sort of hero – but because, apart from knowing every pub within a five-mile radius of our home, he was a heavy drinker and a brawler! My dad, Ray, was over six foot tall, tattooed from neck to ankle, brawny, and he knew how to use his fists. From the age of twenty-two, Dad's crown of thick black hair seemed to disappear rapidly. Nobody messed with him.

The pub was my dad's first home. From an early age, we, as a family, went to the pub. While the adults were inside guzzling, we kids would always be outside with a bag of crisps and bottle of coke. But, if and when something of a stronger brew came our way, it would be down our throats in a second. I can't pinpoint exactly when I developed a strong taste for alcohol, but I knew, from when I was very young, that I liked it.

When I was growing up, I didn't have a lot of interaction with Dad. His day started early, while I was still in bed. When he came home at night, I was in bed again, as he would go straight to the pub from work. I am the eldest of five. My younger brothers looked up to me: they knew I could be relied upon if ever they were in trouble. My sister could have lived in another house, for all the attention we paid her. My mum 'ruled the roost' as far as we children were concerned, but my father pleased himself, and nothing my mother said or did could stop him spending all of his free time in the pub.

One Boxing Day morning really sticks in my mind, and was typical of life in our house. My brothers and I were playing with the gifts that we had received the day before. Mum was pottering about, and my sister was upstairs. It was a nice family Christmas.

'Rose, I'm just popping out for half an hour love,' called Dad.

The whole atmosphere changed as he said those words.

'Don't give me no half an hour, more like all day. Why do you have to go out? Most normal fathers are at home with their wives and kids at this time of year. You have 363 days each year where you can drink yourself stupid,' she shouted.

Smiling, Dad replied, 'Rose, I promise yer, I'll only be half an hour, or three quarters of an hour at the most'.

A torrent of abuse flew out of Mum's mouth, accompanying my dad as he put his cap and jacket on and skulked out of the door. She ran to the door, yanked it open, and flew down the path, hurling abuse at my dad's back. It had no effect. Dad was a man on a mission. Nothing was going to stop him having his bitter!

It was as Mum had predicted. Dad rolled home, well after lunchtime. He must've been the last person to leave the pub. Mum was very angry and verbally abusive, threatening to throw Dad's dinner over his head.

Dad was immune to Mum's mouth, and behind her back he would make faces, which would amuse us children. In fact, the whole situation would amuse us. It happened so often, that we couldn't take any of it seriously.

Alcohol and violence, were the twin evils in my life, from as far back as I can remember. From my early years at school, fighting was the norm. Classes would have pitched battles against each other, in the playground, or in the streets after school. The venue was unimportant.

There was no way that I would let anyone get the better of me. If I had been in a fight my parents would be unsympathetic. Mum and Dad encouraged us to fight back: 'If yer can't hit 'em, kick 'em. If you can't kick 'em, hit 'em with a brick!' they told me. Having that motto drummed into my head, I did as I was told. I started gang fighting when I was as young as five! This violent behaviour, was never seen as being unacceptable. Throughout the East End, being aggressive was a part of growing up – it was life.

My Dad was always ready to fight. It was his way to settle a matter. What would really get him going, was if either his wife or his children were offended. Dad could go from being Mr. Nice Guy, to a complete nutter, in a split-second. One night, outside the Church Elm pub in Dagenham, whilst everyone was saying their goodbyes, Dad thought a guy, who was with a group of men standing nearby him and Mum, had made an improper remark to Mum. Striding purposefully into the group, he head-butted the guy, knocking him to the ground. With fists clenched, he looked around at the remainder of the group, and challenged them. They fled!

It came as no surprise to me, when I learned that a few years before I was born, my father had served a seven-year sentence for violence. It was not unusual for Dad to walk in from the pub, while we were having our tea, covered in cuts and bruises and sporting a black eye. He would go into the kitchen, to have a wash in the sink. His clothes could be literally hanging off his back in shreds, where his opponent had tried to tear them off him. Unperturbed, he would have his tea, and later that evening, would make his way back to the pub, to finish off the fight. The saying, 'Like father, like son', in my case, was very true. Many traits that my dad had, became evident in me.

My time at secondary school, definitely had a positive effect on my life. Firstly, to the shock of my whole family, I passed the eleven-plus. I was shocked. I had not been known for my brilliant intelligence, but achieving a pass in the eleven-plus, allowed me to go to a grammar school. That meant that I only met up with my old mates from Junior school outside school. I now mingled with a different class of people: children who actually wanted to be at school. They talked of what they wanted to do with their lives. Every encouragement was given to them by the teachers. Up to that point, it had never been instilled into me that education was important: school had just been somewhere you went during the day, because it was the law.

The discipline and the strictness of grammar school shocked me. With hindsight, I realise that it was a good environment for a child like me to be in. Robert Clack Technical School, gave me every opportunity to do great things with my life. The shame was that, as I progressed into adolescence, I shunned the very things my teachers were trying to instil in me. It wasn't the school that failed me – I failed them. Many of my teachers put a lot of time and effort into shaping my future, but I blew it. I have nothing but admiration for Robert Clack School – they did their best. Sporting activities, particularly athletics and rugby began to play a big part in my life. Through these two sports, I was able to forge good relationships with my teachers. I was regularly chosen to represent the school at various sporting events. I won medals and certificates. When it came to sprinting and long jump, I usually won the events. I played rugby for the Essex County Schools and I was good. The problem was, that away from all the good that was being input at school, the bad influences that I was getting outside school, began to take a hold.

The six O levels that I attained, helped me to decide to join the sixth form to take A levels.

I was still involved with sports. In the 1974 Essex County Schools Athletics Championships, I was representing my school, as well as the borough of Barking and Dagenham. I won silver medals for the 200 metre sprint, and the 4x100 metre relay. The whole team did really well. On the coach going home, the mood was buoyant.

When we were dropped back at school, some of the other lads asked me if I fancied a drink. They wanted to celebrate. Drinking was already an important part of my life, so I didn't say no. After the first pint they left, but I hung back. There was something special for me, about the atmosphere of a pub. For some people, it might be a pop concert, or for some, the ballet. For me, it was definitely the pub. I have never been a smoker, but the smoky atmosphere, the clinking of the glasses, and the juke-box, made me feel so at home.

Emptying my pockets of all the cash I had, I counted out enough for a few records to be played by the juke-box. By my calculations, I then had enough for four or five pints. The alcohol together with the pride of winning two medals, made me light-headed. I was happy. If I had been the only person in the pub, it would not have worried me. My school friends would have been surprised if they had known that, after they had left the pub to go home, I had sat alone at the bar drinking until my money ran out.

Getting off the bus, and walking towards my house, my excitement was mounting with every step I took. Walking into the house, and seeing my family all together, holding the medals in my hand, and having the beer in my blood stream, brought to the fore the pent-up emotions that were swirling around inside of me. Without saying a word, I burst into tears. Once my family managed to get an explanation out of me, they too were really pleased for me.

After a year in the sixth form, I left. Earning money during the summer holidays, had enabled me to acquire a taste for boozing, nightclubbing and the freedom of doing my own thing. The thought of going back to school to pour over textbooks, learning about subjects that seemed irrelevant to my life, no longer seemed appealing, so school became a thing of the past.

Chapter 2

BOOZING AND BRAWLING

'C'mon son, 'ave another lager.'

The Dagenham Trades Hall was packed. The weekends were all the same. It seemed as though the whole of Dagenham flocked to the Trades Hall, our family included – well my dad and myself. The four pints I'd imbibed were sitting heavily on my stomach, but it didn't stop me from having another one for the road. Guzzling the amber liquid greedily, I looked at my watch.

'I'm off soon Dad, I've got to meet Tony and the others at the Fanshawe at seven.' Draining the last few drops of lager, I patted Dad on the shoulder, put my glass on the bar, and left.

The Fanshawe pub was a dive. The carpet was so dirty, that you could have planted potatoes on it and they would have flourished! There was always a broken window, which allowed the elements to come blowing through; the glasses were always smudged with old lipstick and fingerprints, although, because most of the light bulbs had blown, you couldn't really see – which was convenient for the owners. Yet, I was always there, because of the booze. It was easy to take liberties there, because the owner was past caring. Often, we played cricket in the pub, with a hard ball and things got broken, but no-one cared. Football was another pastime in the pub: not on the toy football machine, but five-a-side, in the main bar! The Fanshawe was a regular sporting pub!

'Ere's your pint Steve', my brother Tony called out to me as I came through the door.

At seventeen, I looked older than I was. Gulping down my sixth pint for the night, I thought, with a smirk that it really was against the law for me to be drinking alcohol in a pub. But who was going to throw me out? The answer was, no-one.

'Right, where are we off to tonight?' I asked.

'I heard that there's a do on at the Church Elm,' piped up Kevin.

'Then that's where we're going, they've got a late licence.'

We drank continuously for the next couple of hours.

The friends that I hung about with regularly, were more like an extended family. We were all of the same mind, and interests. There wasn't much that any of us did outside of our group. All for one, and one for all. Girls did feature now and again, but not to the point where they interfered with the mechanics of the group. Alcohol was the link. Not a day would go by, without all, or at least some, of us meeting up for a good old booze-up.

By the time we came out of the Fanshawe, we had organised ourselves into two car-loads. The two drivers from our gang, had probably put away as much drink as I had, but we didn't think about the dangers of drinking and driving at that time. The Church Elm pub was less than a mile away from the Fanshawe, but we didn't have time to walk, we wanted to save our energy for drinking. The driver of the car I was in, had brought his glass with him. He had one hand on the steering wheel, and the other hand and his lips wrapped around a pint glass. We pulled up about fifty yards away from the Church Elm pub. I was eager to get out and get another pint down my throat. 'C'mon hurry up, open the door,' I shouted.

'Hold on, what's the rush? Have a mouthful of this?' Mickey held out a bag of white powder. I wetted my middle finger in my mouth, and plunged it into the open bag of sulphate. The thick powder, clogged up my mouth. Kevin gave me his glass of lager and I washed the powder down my throat. The rush from the sulphate was instantaneous. I felt like a moon walker, light and carefree. The world seemed a happy place to be in. Laughing and joking, we strutted towards the Church Elm pub.

At the door, the bouncers questioned us. 'Are you all members?'

'Yeah,' we lied.

Because it was 'CB Radio' night, there was a private function going on.

'What is your handle?' he asked us, 'I'll check the list.'

We all burst out laughing. The bouncer was not amused. He knew we were mugging him off. He was just going through the motions. Somebody shouted out, 'Donald Duck', followed by another bright spark who said, 'John Wayne'. We all creased up, it was hilarious.

At that moment, I looked to the left of me, and spied my sister, bawling her eyes out. The smile was wiped off my face, and I rushed to her side.

'What's the matter girl?'

Margaret proceeded to tell me, between tears, that one of the organisers who, incidentally, I had never liked from the day I met him, had literally thrown her out. The reason wasn't too clear, but because he had upset a member of my family, I knew I had to rectify the situation. Pushing past the bouncers, I, my brother Tony and the rest of my mates, stormed up to the bar. My head was spinning like a centrifuge, churning the anger, drink and drugs into a mass. Screaming like a butchered pig, I yelled, 'Where is he?' My voice was loud enough to be heard above the musical strands of 'Dancing Queen'. People stopped and looked at me – I didn't care.

It just so happened, that the person that I was looking for was sitting with a group at the bar, about six feet away from me. He looked at me with horror. My walk turned into a run-up. The last few paces, I flexed myself, balling my hand into a tight, controlled fist, and thumped the guy on the chin with all my might. The force knocked him off the bar stool and onto the floor. He landed a few feet in front of us.

Mayhem, broke out behind me. The bouncers steamed in with weapons, which they used on my mates. The guy was on the floor, semi-conscious. I swung my right foot and began to kick him. He didn't resist, he was out of it. Simultaneously, as a mate of mine smashed a bloke over the head with a bottle, I felt someone hit me across my back with a baseball bat. The blow across my shoulders didn't affect me: it was the end of the blow, which clipped me behind the ear that caused me to fall down on one knee. As I stood up and turned around to sort the geezer out, my brother Tony, who had seen what had happened to me, had taken the bat away from the bouncer and hit him repeatedly with it, until he too fell to the floor. That didn't stop Tony, he continued to hit the bouncer, who by now, was curled up in a ball on the floor, with the wooden bat.

The other two bouncers, were sorted out good and proper by some of my mates, while the remainder of the gang were demolishing the disco equipment, with bar stools. Most people had fled the battle scene by now, but the foolish few who, for some reason, were still hanging about, were being clobbered. They didn't stay around for long! Knowing that the police would soon be on their way. We left.

As we walked towards the car, we began to laugh. The whole episode was funny. It was hard to climb into the motor as, by now, we were rolling about laughing so much. We did not worry at all about recriminations, or the fact that our handiwork, had left at least three people unconscious. The function suite of the Church Elm, would never be the same again!

In the morning, after my excesses of the previous night, I woke up feeling like death warmed up. The blow that I had received to my head had given me concussion. Last night, the lager and sulphate had numbed any feelings of pain – but I was in plenty now! I kept vomiting violently, and was very dizzy. My mate Kevin, whose flat I was staying at, on the Thames View Estate in

Barking, was worried. For him to be so concerned, I must have been bad.

He called an ambulance, which quickly turned up, and took me to the East Ham hospital casualty department. On the way to the hospital, one of the ambulance men said to me, 'If you think you're in a bad way mate, we answered a call at the Church Elm last night. It was a blood bath. Some people are still in Oldchurch hospital as a result.'

He looked at Kevin and I and continued, 'It's a madhouse that pub, do you know it?' Kevin looked at me and smiled. I vomited my stomach contents into a cardboard kidney dish. That was my answer.

At that time in my life, in my early twenties, my drinking was out of control. There just didn't seem to be any limit to how much I could consume in any one day. Working at Ford's as a contractor for a maintenance company, afforded me plenty of opportunities to binge on drink. I was quite friendly with the bosses of the company. It would be common for me to do a few hours work, and then knock off for a few hours and go down to the pub, and indulge myself.

One such time, Big Bill, who was the supervisor for my section, thought he could put me in my place. He was a noted bully, but this particular day he picked on the wrong guy.

'Ere, where 'ave you been?'

I had spent the last couple of hours drinking away a bad night and a bad morning. This was the last thing that I needed. I ignored him.

'Oi, yer deaf or somethin', I'm talkin' to yer.'

I was with a group of my drinking buddies, yet I knew that Big Bill was talking to me. This was his attempt at humiliating me. I gave him a few choice words in reply. This riled him. He walked towards me, swaggering his 21-stone, 6 ft 4 in lump of fat, with the intention of getting me in a bear hug, and sorting me out, good and proper. I had seem him do his 'party piece' on a few occasions.

I was not going to let him do it on me: I was on the defensive. Before he could get a good hold on me, I nutted him square on the nose. He lurched backwards, and landed on his back. His nose was pouring with blood. A few kicks to the head, rendered him semi-conscious. I then returned to the business in hand.

Throughout the rest of my shift, I was fully expecting to be called to the office, and given my cards, but I heard nothing. I could only assume that Big Bill didn't report me. From that day on, I didn't hear a peep out of him. He was as good as gold, the perfect supervisor.

Most days I was in the pub. I had left home to live in a house in Dagenham. I felt adult enough to face the world on my own. The amount of alcohol that I was drinking, didn't worry me. Most of the people that I hung around with drank the same amount, if not more. A lot of people that I knew were dabbling in drugs. I rarely bothered with drugs. And, as I didn't smoke, that wasn't a problem either. I was so used to alcohol, I never found myself reeling in the streets, vomiting all over the place. I was at work regularly (even though I didn't do my full hours) and I was able to communicate competently. There was no slurring of words, or talking incoherently. I would never have associated the words, 'Drunk', 'Wino' or 'Alco' with myself. I was just me: a person who liked to have a good drink every day. The only noticeable effect that alcohol had on me, was that it brought out the violent side of my nature. It wasn't that I needed alcohol to give me courage, I already had plenty of confidence to face the world and his brother! All it seemed to do for me, was give me a nice buzz.

Summer was a time for drinking. Where another person might consume cold, fizzy drinks, or mineral water, I drank ice cold lagers. One particular day, as usual, I had been in the pub since 11 a.m. Outside, the sun was blazing down its hot rays. Most people were outside the pub, sitting at the plastic tables, sipping cold drinks. I was inside, in semi-darkness, propping up the bar, guzzling on my glass that never seemed to run dry.

By six o'clock that evening, I thought it was time that I went home. A few pals of mine and I, had decided to go to a nightclub in Ilford called Barrons. At home I flung a frozen pizza into the oven, while I had a quick shower, and spruced myself up for the evening's adventures.

Barrons, was situated in a big house. It wasn't like the usual run of nightclubs but, for me, it was somewhere where I could indulge myself in my favourite pastime – drinking. The club closed at 2 a.m. Fourteen pints of beer had gone down my throat – I was feeling good. The beer sloshed about inside me, as the cab driver drove me home. At home, I couldn't rest. I still needed a nightcap. There wasn't a drop of booze in my house. I rummaged around the cupboards, for a bit, but I knew that, like Mother Hubbard, my cupboards were bare.

These were not the days of 24-hour supermarkets. The local off-licence was closed and there was no way that I fancied doing a smash-and-grab, just for a drink, even though I felt tempted. Suddenly a light flicked on in my head. Four days earlier, I had purchased a litre bottle of sweet Spanish wine, with a screw-top. The wine was the worst thing I had ever tasted in my life. Now, I would drink most things, but this was truly awful. Some of my drinking buddies had sampled it, and they nearly threw up, it was that bad. Reluctantly, I had put it out with the garbage. Now, I needed it. There was no hesitation. At 3 a.m. I calmly padded to the metal dustbin, which was outside the house, in the front garden. Clad only in my boxer shorts, I began to rummage through the rubbish. The rotten vegetables had turned to slime. Things that were indescribable in shape, texture and colour, but were unified in their smell, were tossed out of the bin, in my determination to get to the bottle. My hand grasped the neck of the bottle, as I yanked it out. It was covered in mouldy baked beans, and potato peelings. I proceeded to unscrew the top, placing the bottle to my mouth. Tilting my head back, I welcomed the thick, sweet liquid, as it flowed through my lips, over my tongue, and down my throat. It was beautiful.

I had attracted an audience of neighbours, who were disturbed by my banging and clattering around in the bin. There was no concern for them, on my part, about all the racket I was making. I just wanted a drink. Once the contents of the bottle had gone, I belched, then tossed it back into the bin, and went to bed. To me, it was just an incident in my life. Nothing special. I needed a drink, and that was the only way to get one at the time!

Chapter 3

FOOTBALL HOOLIGAN

'You put your left leg in, your left leg out, in out, in out, you shake it all about. You do the Hokey Cokey and you turn around, that's what's it all about.' I was singing and dancing on the corrugated metal roof of the main stand at West Bromwich Albion Football club, in the Midlands.

'Get back to your seat, you silly fool,' yelled a policeman.

'. . . Ooooh, the Hokey Cokey,' I taunted the police and the West Bromwich fans beneath me.

The West Ham fans sitting in the seats behind me, and some to my left, who had recognised my claret and blue shirt, cheered me on. I was having a whale of a time.

1986 was the year that I had hoped West Ham would win the league, for the first time ever. It was a bit of wishful thinking on my part, but, you can live in hope! David my brother, and a few friends had decided to hire a minibus, and drive 150 miles north, to support West Ham. We had bought over a hundred cans of lager, and before we even reached the football ground, most of them had gone. We were well tanked up. Out of the four thousand West Ham fans in our particular section, we had managed to muscle our way into the best seats, at the front of the stand. We were overlooking the section of terracing in the main stand, above home fans and the police.

What prompted me to leap over the wall and make an exhibition of myself, was that West Ham had just scored a goal. My confidence in them winning soared. When the West Ham fans, stood up to cheer the team, they also started to sing the Hokey Cokey. I had to go one better.

The police were beckoning me down. I continued to dance up and down, singing off-key, for a few more minutes, with the crowds cheering me on. It was dawning on me, that it wouldn't be long, before the police would nick me, so, with a final wave, I clambered back to my seat.

West Ham won that match. The West Bromwich fans were very subdued, because they had witnessed their team's relegation.

Unfortunately, from our viewpoint, there was no violence that day. We had to find another outlet for our excitement. We waited until we got all the way home to Dagenham, to catch the last couple of hours of drinking time, before the pubs closed.

Football, drinking and fighting, seemed to go together in my life. At many of the football matches that I attended, someone got their head smashed in, or bones broken, or knocked unconscious. Apart from the occasional blow across the back, or a punch in the face, I managed to escape any serious injury to my person.

The Seventies and Eighties were a time when West Ham fans were deemed invincible. No other group of fans could compete against us and win. Being a West Ham fan at that time, was more than supporting a football club, it was like belonging to a very large family. Most of the fans, came from the surrounding areas: east London, Dagenham and some parts of Essex. I felt like I belonged to a tribe. We thought similarly, and our behaviour patterns were identical. I loved everything about West Ham Football club.

*   *   *

' . . . On the charge of grievous bodily harm with intent, how do you find the accused, Mr. Stephen Johnson?'

'Not guilty Your Honour,' said the chairman of the jury.

Turning to face me, the Judge said those beautiful words: 'Mr. Johnson, you are free to go'.

My heart gave a lurch, and I wanted to jump up, and scream out, 'Yes!'

Instead, I nodded my head to say, 'Thank you'. My friends and family in the public gallery were clapping and cheering. The trial had lasted three days. The case had dragged on for eighteen months.

Ironically, I had been playing football, when I got into a fight and I had been stone-cold sober. The next thing I knew, the police were arresting me. A guy in the opposite team, had attacked a friend of mine. My temper flared up, and we had a set-to. It wasn't until the guy ended up in hospital, that the extent of his injuries was realised. That's when the police nicked me. As far as I was concerned, it was self-defence, but my solicitor warned me that I could be looking at seven years behind bars. Was I glad that the jury saw things my way!

Walking through the court grounds, I breathed in the fresh air. I didn't even want to imagine how I would have felt if I had been found guilty. I hadn't realised how precious my freedom was – until then. Patting me on the back, Kevin, my pal said, 'Well done son'. I grinned at him. I had handed him my wallet before I had gone into court, I was half expecting to go down. Now that I was free, I turned to him and said, 'Give us back me dosh, let's go and get drunk'.

My brush with the Law, didn't really have a lasting effect on me. I knew many people that had done one thing or another and had ended up being jailed. It was a fact of life. My lifestyle continued in much the same fashion. I had worked as a bank teller, and in various clerking jobs. I had even done a spot of work labouring on a building site, and working as a sales rep had held my interest for a short while. My work experience was always punctuated by a spell at Fords, as a contractor.

By the late eighties, I was a jack-of-all-trades, but a master of none. I had started a training course, in retail management, for a big company. It was an OK type of job.

'Steve, how do yer fancy being a manager in a carpet shop?' asked Dave Lloyd my brother-in-law. He had seen me flit from job to job: another one wouldn't make much difference.

Laughing, I said to him, 'What do I know about carpets?'

Chuckling, he replied, 'As much as any of us do: don't let that stop you'.

So I began working as a trainee manager for a carpet shop in Plaistow, east London. Within two weeks, much to my amazement, the man who owned the chain of five shops was so pleased with me, that he put me in charge of his biggest shop in Lea Bridge Road, Leyton. I was promoted over his other staff that had been there far longer than I had, not because I was 'Brain of Britain', but because of my keenness, and interest in the job.

I liked the job, but the pay was lousy. I had toyed with the idea of jacking it in, and getting a job that paid more money, but, I managed to supplement my wages by doing a spot of door work. Sometimes I worked for a pub, or if a football club was having a dance, I might be called upon, because of my size, and my reputation for being a guy who could handle himself, to work the door. The arrangement suited me. Having a bit of extra cash in my pocket, I felt I could afford to have myself a good time.

Being in a stable relationship, was not one of my strong points. I liked being out with my mates a lot, and having a girlfriend only cramped my style! Until I met Lisa.

The summer of 1987 was hot. By 11 a.m. one Monday morning, I was bored out of my mind. No-one, it seemed was interested in buying carpets, until two young women, came into my shop. One of them, whose name I found out was Lisa, really caught my eye. She wasn't dressed up, or wearing make-up, but her beauty shone out. Her strong cockney accent amused me, because she was black-skinned. Lisa's bubbly personality brought life into my, otherwise monotonous, day. She ordered a carpet, and I arranged for the estimator to visit her and measure up her flat.

The next few days, was truly a comedy of errors. Suffice it to say, the estimator couldn't organise his way out of a paper bag, so, as a last resort, I had to go to Lisa's flat and sort out her carpet measurements myself. She lived on the 18th floor of a block of flats, on one of the worst housing estates in London. Stepping out of the lift, the smell of stale urine, and the sight of rubbish strewn all over the floor, was sickening. Knocking on her door, I looked around the filthy landing, wishing that I was a million miles away.

As the door opened, my mouth dropped open, and my lungs constricted. I found it hard to catch my breath. Lisa, with her long thick black curly hair, her flawlessly made-up face, and her cute figure, said naturally, 'Hi, come in, I've been expecting yer'. She opened the door even wider and I stepped into her flat.

After measuring up, I sat and chatted with her for over an hour. Her flat was furnished with only the bare essentials, and I could tell that she had only recently moved in. She was buoyant, and seemed to enjoy life.

'. . . So, what part of the West Indies are yer from?' I asked casually, trying to appear cool.

'Well, actually, I'm from Stratford, east London, born and bred.'

I was gobsmacked.

'But my parents are from Mauritius. That's an island in the Indian Ocean, in case yer didn't know,' she continued.

I brushed over my ignorance with a smile (I had thought that Mauritius was in the West Indies).

Reluctantly, I had to go and get back to work. The time I had spent with her, seemed like a minute.

'Well,' I said standing up, 'I'll have to be going now, but I'll make sure that your order gets sorted out quickly.'

Lisa followed me to the door, and as I pressed the button for the lift, she said, 'Pop in for a cup of tea, whenever you're passing'.

Jokingly, I replied, 'Don't say that, I'll be back tomorrow'.

'You're very welcome to.'

I raised my eyebrows.

'No, I really mean it,' she assured me.

The lift came too soon. The door slid noisily closed. My mind was filled with the image of Lisa, at her front door, smiling.

That night, I couldn't sleep. Nothing that I have ever experienced before, had had such an effect on me. I tried to reason with myself that she was just a woman – but, what a woman! I thought about past events in my life – taking exams, fighting in the street, getting blind drunk, even other girlfriends – none of them had ever caused me to lose sleep. The question that stayed with me, until dawn was: did she really mean it when she said 'Pop round again', or was she just being polite?

The next day, I was driving along Forest Road in Walthamstow. At the junction lights, I needed to go straight across. A left turn would have taken me towards Chingford, where Lisa's flat was. Her face came into my mind, throwing my normally calm, decisive mind, into confusion. Should I pop round and see her? Did she really mean it? Is it all a figment of my imagination? Am I going mad? There was no-one that I could have, or wanted to confide in. I had to make my mind up myself. Just as the lights were changing I turned.

Lisa was expecting me, which allayed my fears. After spending several hours talking non-stop, we agreed to start dating.

Within a very short space of time, we were more than an item, we were living together. My consumption of alcohol did not abate, at that time in my relationship with Lisa. She tolerated it – just about. Drinking was part of the package – you got me, you got my boozing.

*   *   *

By 1995, I had graduated to owning my own carpet shop in Hornchurch, Essex. Up until that point, I had continued to float around from one job to another. I had done a stint as a 'minder' for a guy who had various dubious business interests. I drove him around the South East of England. He was loaded with dough: he had a different flash car for every day of the week! I enjoyed driving beautiful sleek motors, and getting good money to do so. Unfortunately, my boss upset me one day, and I had to call it quits. The good thing was, I came away with a good wad of money, and was able to set myself up in my own business.

My social life still evolved around drinking a pub, nightclub, or party dry, and I would often turn very violent as a result. Lisa had seen me involved in violent situations and it did frighten her. But, her love for me was solid (and my love for her was the same) and most importantly, I was never, ever violent towards her.

Business was ticking over nicely. We were living in another council flat in Chingford. By this time we had a son, Martin, who was growing up to be as lovely as his mother.

Throughout the year, I drank a lot. But during the summer months, I consumed twice as much, because of the weather. One particular evening, I decided to go for a few drinks after I shut the shop. I had been drinking cold lagers throughout the day and felt that I needed topping up, before I went home. It was eight o'clock: time to go. Draining my glass, I said goodbye to a few acquaintances that I had got to know through the shop.

Driving down the A406, I was happy and contented with my lot. I was unconcerned that, some years ago, I had been banned for drink-driving. In fact, I wasn't in the least bit worried about drinking and driving and the problems it can cause. I had the window open and my elbow was resting on the van door. Def Leppard was blasting out through my stereo speakers. I was in a hurry to get home and have a bath and something to eat. Lisa is a fantastic cook: she could make a gourmet meal out of a few blades of grass, and an Oxo cube!

My stomach was rumbling, as I pressed harder on the accel-
erator. Glancing in the rear-view mirror, I noticed two motorway
policemen on bikes. Their blue lights were flashing, and the sirens
were going. I was contemplating pulling over to let them through,
when to my horror, I realised that it was me that they were after.
My stomach, which was previously anticipating some good food,
was now turning like a butter churn. I looked down at the speed-
ometer and saw the needle pointing at 86 mph. My heart lurched.
I didn't want to get caught. But, how could I out-manoeuvre them?

In my haste to put distance between them and me, I clipped the
kerb, and nearly rolled the van over the elevated section of the
road, and onto the cars beneath. I shuddered at the thought of what
could have happened. The motorcycled policemen, were now onto
me. One was slowing down in front of my van and the other was
abreast of me, looking through my window.

It took me a while to slow the van down but, eventually, I
pulled into a bus stop, half a mile up the road. Applying the hand
brake, my mind was working overtime. There was no way, I
reasoned to myself, that I was going to get arrested. My drink-
induced muddled thinking was unrealistic. Having watched many
cops and robbers programmes on TV, not to mention James Bond,
I was confident that somehow, I was going to get out of this.

The policeman at the side of me, parked his bike behind me,
and called me out of the van. As I climbed out of the van, I took
in my surroundings. On one side of me was a six-lane carriageway, and to the other was a steep path leading up to the streets
adjacent to the carriageway. I was now in the Woodford area. In
another ten minutes I would have been home. I had to escape.

Out of the corner of my eye, I noted that the policeman was
fumbling in his pockets, probably getting out his notebook. In a
split-second, I legged it up the slope. Quickly glancing back, I saw
one officer drive his bike away from me, presumably in order to
cut me off, further up. Meanwhile the officer who had got off his
bike, jumped back on, and tried to follow me up the path, on his

bike. It took him a while to bump his bike up over the high kerb. That gave me more time to get away.

As I reached the top of the slope, the sound of the revving engine in my ears, was not music. I wasn't far away from being nabbed. Taking a sharp left, I found myself in a dead end. For a moment, I thought, 'That's it, they've got me'.

Three sides of my temporary prison, were garages. There was no way I could get through them. The fourth side, was my only hope. The criss-crossed wiring of the eight-foot-high fence, seemed unclimbable, but I didn't let that deter me. I could feel the policeman's breath against my neck. Taking a deep breath, I leapt up, and I flipped myself over. Because the policeman was so close to me, my foot kicked him in the head. The force of the blow sent the policeman spinning off his bike. I didn't have time to take stock of his plight. Landing on my knees, on the other side of the fence, I found myself, rolling back down onto the road that I had just run away from.

I had to think quickly. There was no way that I would get back into the van. Those coppers would sort me out, make no mistake about it.

In front of me were six lanes of fast moving traffic, separated by a central reservation. At the other side of the road was a 45 ft concrete wall. Where could I go?

Although the policeman I had left behind couldn't see me, I could hear him revving his bike. It wouldn't be long, in my estimation, before he would be 'feeling my collar'.

Without thinking it through properly, I ran across the road. Standing on the central reservation was like being marooned on a desert island. I spied a short, thick bush. Glancing over my shoulder, I ran towards the bush. There was still no sign of the policemen. I dived under the bush. The prickly leaves stuck into my skin. I curled up into the foetal position, and waited. Very soon, I heard motorbike engines roaring up and down the lanes on either side of me. In the distance, and coming closer, I could also hear a police siren. I knew then, it was in my best interest to become a statue – not moving a muscle. I did not want to get caught.

The day was quickly fading. The evening dusk was covering everything in its path. Every car had its headlamps on. By now, a small army of policeman had gathered. I could hear them stripping down my van and I knew I was in for a long wait. All the alcohol I had drunk during the day, had collected in my bladder. I tried desperately to hold on, but I couldn't: I had to let it out. A puddle formed around me, and was soon absorbed into the ground beneath me. I didn't care – I was not moving.

It seemed like a year in time, but was, in fact, about an hour later, when I finally heard the police van drive off. I laid still, in my urine saturated clothes. I had never trusted the Old Bill, and I didn't trust them now. I couldn't hear their voices, or vehicles, yet I wouldn't have been surprised if one or two crafty coppers were still lurking about?

After another hour had passed and the night was pitch black, I tentatively stretched one leg out, slowly followed by the other leg, and then the rest of me emerged from under the bush. I must have been a sight to the drivers on either side of me. That wasn't my problem. I looked across the road: my van had gone. Hitching up my jeans, I prepared to limp the three miles home.

The following morning, I voluntarily gave myself up. I was duly charged for various offences, including having offensive weapons in the vehicle. I got fined a thousand pounds, and I still got a driving ban!

Arthur White

1960, aged 9. Arthur and his mum.

1968, aged 17. With Jacqui at his brother's wedding.

1992, 'Mad Eyes' at the World Championships.

Arthur and Ian at a 'Tough Talk' demonstration and talk.

1988 European Champion.

Arthur and Jacqui on holiday in 1998.

Steve Johnson

Aged 4. Hedgemans Road, Dagenham.

After an 'incident' with a glass.

1995, in party mood.

Steve and his dad.

Ian McDowall

Aged 18. Training at Wag's gym, East London.

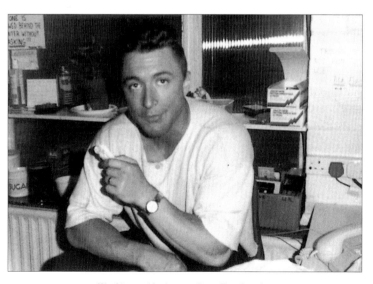

Working at Alan's gym, Bow, East London.

'Posing' at the age of 20.

Getting baptised at Canning Town swimming pool.

Chapter 4

59 STITCHES!

' . . . When he wakes up, tell him not to come back here, get it,' I shouted after a group of guys who were carrying their unconscious friend out. My boss (in his absence) had been verbally abused by him. There was no way I was going to stand by, and have someone I knew and respected, insulted, so, I battered the guy until he passed out.

I was working, at the time, as a bouncer at the Church Elm pub. The money supplemented my wages, and the drinks were free. Chucking troublemakers off the premises, and beating up anyone who deserved it, fitted in with my violent persona. I remember that particular night, back in December 1994, very well. As per usual, I had been drinking all day long. My favourite drink at the time was called a 'Purple Paratrooper'. It consisted of half a pint of lager, half a pint of cider and a shot of Pernod, with a drop of blackcurrant to give the drink a nice colour. It was a lethal combination. In some public houses, mixing lager and cider together – which is called 'Snakebite' – is banned. It was 1 a.m., and because I was a member of staff, I could drink what I liked. Whenever I drank a Purple Paratrooper it would have an adverse effect on me. The guy that I had thrown out would have felt every punch that I threw. When he came round, I knew that he would remember me!

It was a regular event to be having a 'late' drink with the owners of the pub. I could stay in a pub, all night and all day, drinking. Half an hour later, I was feeling good. The after hours drinking was popular, and there were about fifty people, like me, who enjoyed a good drink. My left hand was in my pocket, and my right was attached to my glass. I was totally unprepared for what happened next. I heard a 'pop' sound, as my head was thrown backwards. My eyes were closed, but I could feel that my face was covered with a warm, sticky liquid. I realised straight away what had happened. I had been hit in the face with a glass. The mate of the guy I had previously slung out, had come back for revenge.

Opening my eyes, I realised that my right eyelid was hanging down in front of my eyes, by a thread. My left eyelid was sliced across the middle. People were screaming, 'He's lost his eyes'; another shouted, 'He's been blinded'. All around me was bedlam. Bar towels were being placed over my face, to mop up the blood. Blood was pouring from my face from seven different places. The torrent of blood that was flowing down my eyes didn't stop me from seeing. Even though I could literally only see red, I knew I hadn't been blinded. People around me, led me to a chair. I sat down waiting for the ambulance to come. I still had my drink in my hand.

The outcome of the evening's events, was that I had to have 59 stitches in my face. My feelings and plans for revenge were more a matter of principle, rather than anything personal. I didn't hate the guy, but what he had done to me, was well out of order. He had to be sorted out.

I was never able to catch the guy who scarred my face. He proved to be very elusive. A couple of years later, I heard, on the grapevine, that he was found hanging in his cell in a secure mental institution.

My employers were very serious people. Working for them on a regular basis, I found myself involved in more and more dodgy dealings. My colleagues were the sort of men who thought nothing of carrying a gun at all times, like some people carry an umbrella!

Drink often brought out the worst in me. My temper had always sprung to the fore in an instant. Alcohol made it even worse. My need for drink at times seemed more important than my need for oxygen.

I would often spend days away from Lisa. It wasn't because I loved her less, but because the combination of drinking from morning to night, and working unsociable hours, did not promote a loving relationship. My life was taking a nose dive.

Very rarely would I sit and reflect on my life. I was usually too full of drink to do that. But, on the odd occasions that I did, I began to realise that something was wrong with my life. To tell you the truth, it wasn't a life. I was just existing from one mad, drunken, violent situation to another. But I pushed those thoughts out of my mind quickly. There wasn't really anything I could do to stop the direction that I was going in. I would think about giving up drinking occasionally, but within an hour, I would be back drinking again. There was no solution.

My wife Lisa is a woman in a million. Throughout all my wild drinking bouts, she didn't berate me continually about my alcohol consumption. But, there were times when she would draw the line.

'. . . Please Steve, I'll have all the food ready for eight. You know I don't ask you for much, so please be on time.'

'No problem love, expect me at eight, I'll be home then.'

I had been working all day. As usual, I had spent quite a bit of time in the pub. Now it was summer, drinking cold lagers was my excuse to keep cool. This particular day that Lisa expected me home early, was no exception. It had been on my mind all day, to get home for eight and I had deliberately left work early. Two hours, in fact. About a mile from where we lived, was a pub called The Royston Arms. It was a place that I frequented in order to have a few more drinks before finally going home.

I got to the pub for 6 o'clock that evening. I reasoned that I would have been home far too early for Lisa, and would have probably got in her way, as she was preparing our meal. One hour of solid drinking later, I espied Maestro's wine bar across the road. My friend Mark was the owner. I usually drank in the Royston, until Maestro's opened at 7 p.m. I thought to myself that as I had another hour to kill. I might as well spend it there. The scorching sun, mingled with the large volumes of lager I had drunk that day, caused sweat bubbles to pop up all over me. I needed to replace the liquid I was losing.

Mark opened the doors of his wine bar: I was his first customer. Wayne was the barman at Maestro's, and he and I had become sort of pals.

' . . . Steve, nice to see yer. I've got good news for yer.'

'What's that then?' I asked.

Bending down behind the bar, I thought he was going to play some trick on me, but instead, he came up with a crate of beer in his hands, and plonked it down on the bar.

'Yer said the beer wasn't strong enough in here for yer, so we got these in especially for you.'

'Oh, nice one Wayne.'

I was pleased with the bottles of beer. They were Pils lagers: very potent, just how I liked my beer. It was true, I was forever complaining about the weakness of the beer. The cool, dry tasting lager flowed quickly across my tongue, and down my throat. The next eight bottles tasted just as good as the first. Within the space of two hours I had drunk thirteen pints of alcohol. The effect of all those drinks, made me feel on top of the world. I wasn't far from home, and I would please Lisa in being back for eight.

Driving home, tanked up to the hilt, a thought slowly crept into my mind. Was I addicted to alcohol? Most days, in fact every day, I drank. The amounts varied from five pints to fifteen per day. Was that normal? I shook my head to clear it. It was a stupid thought, and I didn't want it in my mind anymore.

When I got home Lisa was surprised: 'Well done mate, you've got here on time.'

I grinned.

As Lisa dished up the food, I got a few bottles of beer out of the fridge.

'I might as well have a little drink with my meal.'

'Alright love, you're probably a bit thirsty,' she said with a twinkle in her eye.

Maestro's became my favourite haunt. Nearly every evening, whether just for an hour or so, or longer, would be spent having a drink there. Wayne, Mark and I became good friends. So much so, that Mark and I decided to go into business together. Besides the wine bar, Mark already owned a plumbing shop, and a promotions company.

There was a dilapidated shop, a few doors away from the wine bar. I had noticed the shop, and Mark knew that I was looking for premises locally.

'Shall we try for that Steve? We can buy it together and you could use the shop for your carpets, and the upstairs we could rent out. What do you say?'

It sounded feasible to me. I agreed.

It worked out quite well really – we were going to sub-let the flat, and share the income. I would run the carpet shop as my own business, but I also agreed to give Mark a proportion of the rent for a shop in Chingford. This was because he jointly owned the building. The mortgage would be shared. As far as I could see this would work out fine, for the both of us. Months were spent grafting, down in the shop, getting it ready. But money has a funny way of changing once solid friendships.

In the weeks leading up to the shop being ready for business, Mark kept hinting about actually having a share of the carpet business (which was my private enterprise) as well as all the other things that we jointly shared. I was put out, to say the least. My interpretation of his request was: he saw me as a drunken mug, a soft touch. He had seen me in action – fighting and drinking and going crazy, and thought that I didn't have much 'upstairs'. Well, he was wrong.

It all came to a head, the second Saturday that the shop was open.

'Yer still haven't signed this contract Steve, what are yer playing at.'

He had stormed into the shop with a cigar hanging out of his mouth. I think he thought he was the 'Godfather' of Chingford or something! He had been trying to get me to sign his dodgy contract for a while, and I had been blanking him. Today was different.

My brother-in-law Dave, was having mid morning coffee, when he witnessed me losing my cool. Mark was leaning across the desk, waving his finger in my face, and speaking very disrespectfully to me.

'. . . Don't shout at me, otherwise you'll see a side of me that you won't like,' I warned him.

He didn't listen.

I moved with speed. Hooking my fingers into the front of his shirt, I simultaneously pulled him towards me and slashed at his face with a Stanley knife. My brother-in-law nearly choked on his coffee. Instinctively, Mark leapt back, and I missed his nose by an inch. Terror replaced aggression as Mark visibly paled and backed his way out of the shop. I rushed from behind my desk and chased him. He narrowly missed colliding with a fruit and vegetable stall. He ran for safety into his plumbing shop and locked the door. I didn't waste time trying to break down the door: I knew I would see him again. Soon.

Wayne, was my lodger in the upstairs flat. He too, had underestimated me. Because I saw him as a friend, I had overlooked his non-payment of the rent. Now things had changed. To my mind, Wayne had not been a great tenant. Because of the bad business with Mark, I decided he had to go. After a fire in the flat, that was definitely the final straw. The trouble was, apart from having to repair the flat myself, Wayne owned me money – and I wanted it.

One Saturday night, I was on my way to a local boxing match with my mate, Eddie. We decided to have a quick drink before we got to the gym where the match was being held. After Eddie had brought us a pint each, I casually glanced around me, and noticed a crowd of about fourteen or fifteen blokes at the end of the bar, being very boisterous, loud and mouthy!

Among this rowdy lot, I noticed Wayne. Our eyes met and, like a snake, he wiggled his way over to me. I wasn't happy to see him, but, he seemed confident of himself, as he had his mates to back him up. He approached me, with his mouth running like an out of control motor engine, and started giving me some cock and bull story about his financial problems. Did I really care? In a word – No!

'Get lost,' I sneered.

Wayne, being a bit thick-skinned, continued to hassle me. I knew he had to be dealt with, quickly and simply. My hand lashed out so fast, that Eddie didn't even see it. My fist made contact with Wayne's chin. He crashed to the floor backwards, to the shock of his mates. I took a sip from my glass, totally unruffled. Nodding to Wayne's friends, I said, 'Get rid of him, he's fouling up the place'.

They picked him up, like a sack of potatoes, and took him outside. His mates came back in and acted as though it never happened. That was fine by me.

A few weeks later, I was visiting a gym not far from where I lived. As it happened, one of the guys that was present the night I socked Wayne in the chin, was there too. This bloke, who was noted for being the 'hard man on the firm', came to me and said, 'Steve, can I 'ave a word with yer?'

We were half-way up the stairs at the time and, for an instant, I thought the guy was going to pull a fast one. If he had, I wouldn't have hesitated in throwing him down the stairs, head first. But what he said next surprised me.

'Listen mate, I know that you've been making Wayne's life a misery lately. Well, he's working for me now.'

I tensed up, ready to strike, thinking that the guy was going to say something like, 'So, if yer have any problems with Wayne, yer have to go through me, right'.

But, he continued, 'How much does he owe yer? Tell me, and I'll sort it out'. He placed his hand over his pocket.

I paused, taking in the information. I laughed: 'For a start, it was only ever the principle, rather than the money, anyway. I didn't want anyone thinking I was an idiot, and that they could take liberties with me.'

'We know we couldn't do that to yer Steve.'

'Well, in that case, forget the thousands that Wayne owes me. Send him into my shop, to apologise, and I'll accept fifty quid. That way, I can take my wife out for a meal, and the whole thing is forgotten.'

The geezer was well chuffed. He shook my hand and said, 'Steve, I could make Wayne pay yer off'.

Shaking my head, I said, 'Forget it. I just wanted to prove a point.'

I have to say, the guy was true to his word. Wayne turned up the next morning bright and early. An apology rolled off his lips, followed by fifty quid out of his pocket. We shook hands on a gentlemen's agreement. I promptly went and spent the lot down the pub.

* * *

Days of my life, at that time, passed by in a haze. My life was like a leaf blowing in the wind. Somehow, I had got detached from the rest of the human race, and I was floating about by myself.

I had several so-called 'best friends'. The truth of the matter was that they were really only drinking buddies. If it wasn't for the booze, I probably wouldn't have passed the time of day with them.

Time had no meaning for me. As far as I was concerned, life in its totality was shared between the pub, or wine bar and home, with a little bit of entertainment on the side. I could never have got through the day without a drink. I didn't consider myself to be a drunk, but at times, when I just had to have a drink, and went into a pub and whiled away the hours with only a pint glass for company, I would wonder to myself if this was normal. Anyway, I reasoned, I was no psychologist. What was the point of bashing out my brains, trying to analyse my every thought or action?

I continued to drink heavily. It was my one enjoyment – so, why not enjoy.

Chapter 5

SET FREE

I had never met a born-again Christian in the flesh, until the summer of 1995. That's when I first met Alan Mortlock. The closest I have ever come to a Christian was the vicar, either at a wedding or a funeral. The only other person I knew of who was one, and it was never in the flesh, was Cliff Richard on the telly! So, when a tattooed man, with a shaven head, clad only in shorts and a vest, burst into my carpet shop in Chingford, and into my life, I was knocked for six.

After introducing himself, he gave me spiel about what he was about.

'My name's Alan Mortlock, and I own the gym up the road. I'm looking for local businesses to sponsor a kick-boxing event, that is going to be held in my gym.'

My ears pricked up, at the word boxing. 'Oh yeah,' I said, 'tell me more.'

So he did.

'If yer give me thirty quid, yer'll be entitled to free advertising in the programme. Also, some ringside seats, free of charge. What do you say to that then?'

'Where is it?'

When he told me, I thought that it would be an event that I would like to see. I knew that the place had a bar, and the drinks were cheap.

'I'll 'ave some of that.' I handed him the money.

Over the next few minutes, we sort of shared our backgrounds. I let him know that I could handle myself: that I was nobody's mug. I could see him wince, when I recounted a few tales, but, I wanted to reinforce the fact that I didn't mess about. It also came out in the conversation that I was almost permanently in the pub. He must have sussed that my life had 'lost the plot', and that my only aim in life was to drink, drink, drink.

Alan, to my mind, was of a similar calibre. He seemed to know a lot of the people that I mentioned and to know them, he must have been OK. We shook hands, and Alan walked off towards the door. He was just a few feet from the door, when he turned and said to me: 'Steve, can I take another five minutes of yer time'.

I shrugged and said, 'Yeah, of course'.

'I was a bit like you once' he said. 'I had an eight-year cocaine addiction, and I was a boozer like yer as well. But something drastic changed my life.'

I didn't know why he was telling me all this. Besides, as far as I was concerned, my life was alright, and it didn't need changing. Politely, I said 'Go on mate, tell me about it, what changed yer life'.

His answer floored me. 'Jesus Christ.'

I felt as though I had been bashed with a brick. My mind leapt in different directions at once, throwing me into confusion. My very first thought was – the geezer has got to be mad. This guy, covered from head to foot in tattoos, was not my idea of a born-again Christian. Gritting my teeth, because I didn't want to upset him too much, I wished that I hadn't been so quick to hand over my money. To make matters worse, instead of leaving me alone, he pulled up a chair and sat down, making himself at home, and proceeded to tell me about Jesus, and the miracles he had seen. I smiled, and thought – this geezer is definitely out of his tree. There's a light on, but no-one's at home. I was tempted to ring up the emergency services, and have him carted off to the funny farm. He was one strange guy!

Two weeks passed. I went along with some of my pals, to the kick-boxing event, and got as drunk as a skunk. I had a great time. Over the next few weeks, I was glad that Alan had come into my life, because the bar attached to the gym, was mega cheap, it became my local. He had done me a big 'miracle'!

As I began to frequent Alan's gym, I discovered that all that he had said about his past life was true. He had many friends and people that had known him, in his bad old days, who told me that he was a completely changed man. I digested everything that was said, and compared it to the Alan that I knew. Still, his lifestyle had no appeal: I decided that it was not for me.

Several months had passed, since I first met up with Alan. He would pop into my shop now and again, and I would see him at his gym. I didn't go for any recreational activity, other than drinking! In fact, we became good mates.

It was a week before Christmas, when I had a bit of an accident. I had been calculating how many carpets I needed to fit, in order to give my family and myself a good Christmas. I knew that carpet fitting would never make me a millionaire, and I had been doing a few dodgy dealings, as well as door work, on the side, to bump up my earnings. Lifting carpets was part and parcel of my job. The carpet fitter and I were trying to lift a full roll of carpet, weighing several hundred pounds into the back of the van. I was able to hold my end up, but the carpet fitter couldn't hold his. He dropped it. Unfortunately, the full weight of the carpet went onto my shoulders, jarring my back and forcing me down onto my knees. The guy was useless. He stood still, transfixed, as I struggled to get up off the floor. I staggered over to where he had dropped the carpet on the ground, and hoisted it up onto the van. I had to walk back to my end of the carpet, and push the carpet, with all of my might, until the whole of it was in the van. As I was doing this, I knew that I had seriously injured my back, and that in making sure that the carpet was safely in the van, I had complicated the injury.

The pain was unbearable. I couldn't think straight, let alone walk straight. Sitting down was agony, yet, standing up was no better. I needed some medical help. I had no option, but to lock up the shop. It was early afternoon. At that time of the year shutting up the shop early meant a big loss of earnings, but what could I do?

I didn't want to seek medical help: I hadn't been to see a GP in ten years, and the only time I had been to hospital was to be stitched up. Bed was my answer to the terrible pain that seemed to be tearing my back apart. In fact, the pain was radiating throughout my whole body: there didn't seem to be a single part of it that didn't hurt! As I lay in bed, I knew that the next morning the pain was going to be a hundred times worse. It was!

I didn't know what to do, but one thought kept coming to me – I've got to open the shop. Dressing myself proved to be more than I could manage by myself. Lisa, my wife, had to help me. I was like a baby, as she slipped on my socks and shoes, and helped me to button my shirt. I had never been in such a state before. I limped to my car, and I don't know how I managed to drive it the two miles to work.

The shop was already open. A team of builders were carrying out some repairs, and I had given them the key to let themselves in. As I gingerly made my way to my desk, the pain was intense. This was a heavy scene I was going through. Sweat was pouring off my brow. I had to hang on to the doorposts, as I tried to navigate myself into my chair – no can do! I couldn't sit down. The builders, were half concerned, half laughing at the state I was in.

I didn't know what to do when the phone rang. It was Alan for one of the builders. After he had finished speaking to one of them, he wanted to speak to me.

'Hello mate,' I said.

'Hello son, yer don't sound too good.'

I told him about my back injury.

Without hesitation, he said, 'Yer need the Lord'.

'I need a doctor – yer need a psychiatrist,' I replied.

He was absolutely serious. He said quietly, 'Yer need prayer'.

I told him straight. 'Look Alan mate, I'm not in the mood for all that kind of talk today.'

Ignoring me, he said, 'I'm coming down the shop to pray with yer'.

Horrified, I told him, 'I don't want yer showing me up in public. I don't want yer here.'

'I'm going to pray for yer son. If yer don't let me come down there, then yer'd better come here. Either way, I'm going to pray for yer and now.'

The pain was making my mind swim in and out of numbness. I didn't have the energy to argue with him. I reasoned that it would be less embarrassing if I went to his place. After replacing the handset, I limped and shuffled my way the 400 yards or so to his gym. When I entered his office, Alan said to me, 'Hello son, the Lord's going to heal yer today'.

I was not in the mood for joking, and pointless chatter. I told him, 'Get on with it Al, I've got a lot of things to do'.

Standing in the middle of the room, doubled up in pain, I let Alan place one hand on my head, and the other on my back.

'Steve, the Lord's told me to tell yer, he's going to heal yer now.'

I was not impressed, and thought to myself: does this 100 per cent fruit and nutcase expect me to believe, that 'the Lord' talks to him, and especially, about me? He needed certifying. I just nodded my head, to keep him happy.

'Lord,' said Alan, full of confidence that the Lord was hearing him. 'Lord, I know that I have no power; but yer do. I know that yer have got yer hand on Steve's life, but he doesn't believe it yet. I ask yer to relieve this pain, in the Name of Jesus. I ask yer Lord Jesus to heal his back, in the Name of Jesus. Let Steve know that yer alone perform miracles, today, just as yer did 2,000 years ago. Amen.'

Alan said to me, 'Steve, I believe yer will be 95 per cent healed straight away, and that by the morning, yer will be 100 per cent perfect'.

Smiling, more to humour him, than for anything else, I said, 'See yer later'.

It was only as I was bouncing down the stairs, leading from his office to the street, that it hit me – I was no longer in terrible pain. Confusion was trying to find a resting place in my mind, like a bee on a flower, but, I refused to let it take me over. I pushed my back injury, and Alan, forcibly out of my mind, and got on with the rest of my day.

Lisa was amazed when I got home. 'Yer left here in agony this morning, and now you're as fit as a fiddle.'

Shrugging my shoulders, I told her about Alan.

'Oh right!'

We had our evening meal, and forgot about it. That night I went to bed, with a bit of stiffness. The next morning, just as Alan had said it would happen, I was totally pain-free.

That Christmas was as good as ever. The reason for the Christmas break didn't concern me. It was a time to indulge in gluttonous behaviour, drunken revelry, and shop-'til-you-drop greed.

The New Year brought an excuse to drink as much as my stomach could expand to. At the gym, I would be having my usual number of pints. One late morning, mid-week, as I walked past Alan's office on my way to the bar, I could hear a lot of hooting and hollering. I knew it was one of Alan's prayer meetings, and I tried to sneak past. Just as I thought I had escaped to the bar, Alan saw me through the half opened door.

'Stevie, how are yer doing?'

I was gutted that he had caught me, before I managed to get my throat wet.

'Alright mate.' My half-hearted response, didn't put him off.

'There's a few people I want to introduce yer too.'

With him in the office were two big, big geezers, who he introduced to me as his 'brothers in Christ'. Another mad lot I thought. But, what struck me was that they looked normal. They were pub bouncers. They didn't look like my idea of born-again Christians. I always thought Christians, were wimps. I wouldn't have wanted to take my chances bumping into these two down a dark alley!

Before I knew it, they were all laying hands on me, and praying for me. I couldn't escape. When they had finished communicating with Heaven on my behalf, I politely said, 'See yer' and went over to the bar, and had six or seven pints. I pushed the incident to the back of my mind. I knew Alan had my interests at heart, but I just wasn't up for it.

Three weeks later, I was drinking yet again in the bar, with some of my boozing cronies, when Alan called me over. He handed me a brown paper bag. Handling it, it felt like a heavy box of chocolates, but I couldn't work out who would give them to me. Alan solved the mystery.

'Do yer remember those geezers who prayed with you a few weeks ago,' he said, 'one of them sent it for you.'

As I opened it up, I saw the purple lettering – 'THE BIBLE'. I shoved it back quickly into the bag. I was nervous in case any of my mates saw it. I slipped it into one of my jacket pockets. I was wearing a Levi denim jacket. The pockets were so deep, you could have hidden the Crown Jewels in them. In one pocket, I had a can of CS gas. In the other pocket I had a policeman's cosh, and now a Bible! Though the Bible was well concealed, I was conscious of it in my pocket. Even though my pals and I had visited various drinking holes, and I was merry, to say the least, I didn't want anyone of them getting an inkling of what I was carrying.

I didn't reach home until three in the morning. I handed Lisa a bag of cold curry in one hand, and in the other, the brown paper bag, containing the Bible. She was half asleep, and angry that I had woken her up. Holding out the Bible to me, she said, 'What do yer want me to do with this?'

Slurring I replied, 'I don't know. Some geezer gave it to me. But whatever yer do, don't bin it.'

Over the next few months, although my life hadn't changed one
iota, I would pick up the Bible now and again and read a bit of it,
as a source of comfort. I didn't understand a lot of it, but, I found
that the Psalms and Proverbs helped soothe my mind.

*   *   *

Autumn. Alan called me one day out of the blue. 'What are yer
doing Sunday morning?'

'Lying in bed with a hangover as usual,' I replied.

He laughed. 'You've heard about a bloke called Jimmy Tibbs?'
he said.

'Yes.'

I knew that Jimmy Tibbs was an ex-villain from Canning Town,
and he was also Nigel Benn, the Boxer's trainer. He had also been
associated with one of my cousins in the boxing world.

'Well, he's going to be telling his life story, at a local hall. Do
yer want to come along?'

I told him I would.

Alan and I agreed to meet up at his gym. Alan had also arranged
to meet with a couple of other guys, who were ex-boxers and now
pub bouncers. We shook hands, and then left by car, to go to the
hall. I felt at ease in their company. One of the guys, Es Kaitell, I
had already met before, through Alan. Although I realised Es was
a born-again Christian, I still didn't realise that they were actually
taking me to church. The church was being held in a school hall!

Walking through the door of the hall, a few minutes late, it
dawned on me we were going into a church meeting of some kind,
but I was fine about it, because the people seemed to be happy,
and enjoying themselves. The music was toe-tapping and hand-
clapping good. The instruments that were being played, would not
have been out of place in a rock band! I had expected a pipe organ
– this was very new for me.

I listened to Jimmy Tibbs tell his life story. He said the same thing that Alan had said, in that, when he gave his life to Jesus, he had changed. I was able to speak to him after the meeting. He seemed like a guy that was well in control of his faculties. He didn't appear to be brain-washed, he was still a 'man's man'. He stood by the fact that he claimed to have a personal relationship with Jesus Christ. I was impressed.

Christmas 1996 was around the corner. Sitting on a bar stool, propping myself up, I drank, and drank, pint after pint. I was a lonely, sad bloke. Hanging around with the men that I did, my drinking pals, was not only boring me, but there seemed to be something awakening in me that was telling me it wasn't right. I had more and more, over recent weeks, separated myself from these guys. Life with them wasn't fun anymore. I seemed to meet up with born-again Christians, time after time, but for the life of me, I just couldn't see myself going that way. I was the type of person who spoke volumes with my fists. I didn't suffer fools gladly. How could I, I thought, ever fit in with these people. Never. Yet, my life was bare. I didn't seem to fit in anywhere. I would be drinking myself into oblivion, when really, I should have been at home, like most normal men, with my wife and children, enjoying being a family man. I couldn't. Drink came first.

Envy was uppermost in my mind, when I thought about Alan, Es and the others, whose lives had once been as messed up as mine was, but now had been transformed by Jesus. But I didn't want Jesus to do it for me. Here I was, a fully grown man. Husband, father, self-employed businessman. I was out there doing it – yet, somehow, my life wasn't matching up to all those positive images. Try as I might, I couldn't get the pieces to hold together. It was hard, keeping myself on the rails. Every couple of steps I would fall off, and end up back at square one! I would not admit defeat and call out for help. I wanted to do things my way, or no way at all! Evaluating my life, I began to see a pattern. Just as I would be on the threshold of accomplishing something worthwhile, I would fail. Fall flat on my face. With brute strength,

I would pick myself up, brush myself down, and start all over again. It didn't matter what I was attempting: school, work or relationships, the results were always the same. The constant failure led me on a course of self-destruction – big time.

Christmas was a day or two away. I had made up my mind that I wasn't going to keep the company I usually kept, in order to enjoy a drinking bout. But, I wasn't strong enough to say no. I found myself preparing to go out to meet up with them, purely, because I needed a drink! Getting dressed in my bedroom, I thought it was madness that here I was, getting ready to associate myself with people I didn't really want to be with.

Out of the blue, I found myself praying: 'Jesus, I know deep down, that it was you who healed my back. And that it is you that has changed the lives of all the people I have met. Please change mine. Take this drink thing away from me. I'm sick and tired of the life I am leading. Please help me.'

Jesus heard me. That night, for the first time in my life of drinking, I found myself unable to drink. Whereas before, I would never refuse a drink, and would spend the whole night constantly guzzling at the bar. This night was different.

Within an hour and a half, I passed through the doors of three or four different public houses. In each of them the same thing happened. I would have a drink put in front of me, and the most I could take from each glass was a sip. The feeling was strange. The company was boring. My desire for alcohol, had mysteriously gone. In my confusion I returned home early, and sober.

Lisa was shocked.

'Are you ill,' she asked, looking at me as though I had grown two heads.

'No love, I think I've got things sorted.'

Christmas came and went. I didn't get sloshed once. In actual fact, I didn't even fancy a drink! This was my own personal miracle.

Between Christmas and the New Year, I phoned Alan up and

asked him if he was going back to that church, where he had previously taken me to see Jimmy Tibbs.

'Yeah, I'm going to the Way In Christian Fellowship. Why? Do yer want to come?'

'Yeah, I do,' I replied.

The atmosphere of the church moved me physically and emotionally. I can't clearly recollect what the pastor, Simon Smith, spoke about, but the words sunk in deep into my being. I was moved to tears. At the end of the service, he asked people to come forward, if they wanted to surrender their life to Jesus. Several people went forward. I wasn't one of them. Whether it was pride, fear, or arrogance, I don't rightly know. I was rooted to my chair. Alan sensed that I wanted to go, but for some reason, couldn't. He looked at me and said,

'Yer alright son?'

I said, 'I think so mate'.

'Do yer want to speak to me afterwards, in the office?'

I nodded.

In the office, memories from the past, such as being prayed for, receiving the Bible, and getting drunk, flooded into my head. Without wasting anymore time I told Alan, 'I want to commit my life to Jesus'. He led me in a simple prayer, asking God to forgive me of my evil ways, and accept Jesus Christ as Lord, and Saviour. Alan also asked the Lord to guide me, in my life from then on.

*   *   *

Three years have passed since that day. Unlike other people, who may have had a drink addiction, and are advised never to drink again. I, by the power of the Name of Jesus, now have control over whether I have a drink or not. I could go to a pub, and not be tempted to have a drink. And if I did have a drink, I would be able to stop. Now, I drink less in a year, than I used to drink in a week!

Aggressive confrontations, used to be daily occurrences. For me, that was the answer to any problem that arose. To swiftly deal with people, with a punch in the mouth or verbal abuse, was the way to settle disputes. That type of behaviour is truly a thing of the past. My family life has been strengthened by God's love. Every business transaction is legitimate.

I cannot undo any of the bad things I have done in the past. Shame overwhelms me when I think of some of the things I did. Drink-driving, is something that causes me to shudder. To think, that I used to believe that I could safely handle a car, when my bloodstream was full of alcohol: it was sheer madness.

These snapshots of my life, are just examples of what I was like. For most of my life, I had attempted, in my own strength, to lead a good life. Because it was in my own strength, I could never succeed. I feel great remorse over the broken relationships and broken lives I have caused. I can't turn back the clock.

However, I now have a power and a love to help me through any situation. Although it doesn't mean my life is a bed of roses, I now have access to a strength and a peace that surpasses anything imaginable. This power, love, strength and peace, I cannot and will not stop talking about. This is my Lord and Saviour, Jesus Christ.

IAN McDOWALL

Chapter 1

PUMPING IT UP

'Ughhhhhhhhh!'

'C'mon Ian, you can do it, one more rep,' shouted Gary.

Doing squats with a 400 lb barbell, was like carrying the weight of the world on my shoulders. I wanted to stop.

'Don't give up Ian. Uppppp!' Tony bellowed in my ears. My whole body felt like a ton of lead. Every muscle was protesting against the onslaught of the gruelling regime I was putting my body through.

'400 – you've done it!' said Tony clapping me on the back.

I collapsed on the floor, drenched in sweat, but pleased that I had accomplished what I had set out to do.

Every day I gave myself goals to be achieved. No matter how hard or how difficult they were, I wouldn't feel good unless I reached them.

Slowly, I eased my 5 ft 8 in, 17-stone bulk up off the floor, and made my way to the changing rooms.

The weather was bang on target for Christmas Eve – inside the gym and out. In the changing rooms, for as long as I had worked there, a window had been broken, and never repaired. Goose-bumps appeared all over me like a rash.

'I reckon the only way that window is gonna get sorted, is if I do it myself,' moaned Tony.

'Yeah, Allan's so tight, if you got it done, he'd probably dock yer wages,' I laughed. Tony grinned, he knew exactly what I meant. Allan was the owner of the gym, and to say that he didn't like to spend money, was an understatement!

The hot shower livened me up. The jets of water massaged my aching muscles.

' . . . What yer say Tony?' I could just about hear him, over the sound of the shower.

'I said,' yelled Tony, 'do yer want me to get yer the gear or not?'

My shower stopped, and I began to dry myself. The very question that Tony had asked me had been running around my mind for some time. The 'gear' that Tony was referring to was anabolic steroids.

I had already been taking an eight-week course of steroids in tablet form. From the time I started weight training, when I was about fourteen years old, I had toyed with the idea of taking steroids: but, I had resisted. Even though lots of people around me were chucking them down their throats, or injecting them, I thought it was cheating. I took the first course because I was fed up of losing. Because I was so obsessed with my body and with winning, it was very hard for me to keep getting a knock-back. I knew from the last competition that I had entered, and lost, that things would have to change. The very first tablet that I washed down with water, gave me an instant feeling of euphoria. Not because of the effect of the tablet, but because it gave me a psychological high in knowing the effect that the steroids would have on my appearance, and performance in the long run.

The first competition that I entered after I started taking the steroids, was in Portsmouth. It was a big affair for me. When my name was called out as the runner-up, I wanted to jump, and yell and scream out 'Yes'. Instead, ever Mr. Super Cool, I casually raised my hand, and sauntered towards the platform, where I collected the first of my many trophies.

Coming out of the shower, Tony's voice followed me as I

walked to my locker.

'Well, do yer or don't yer?'

I pulled my jeans on, and answered: 'To tell you the truth Tony, I feel ready now to start taking some injectables, but, it's the hundred quid mate. I can't find it on Allan's wages.'

Tony laughed: 'Yer right, we can just about afford a Big Mac on what he pays us.' Walking out of the gym into the cold early evening air, Tony and I laughed about the wages Allan paid us. But, never one to lose the thread of a conversation, Tony continued to plague me about the gear.

'Look, I would love to say to yer "Ian, here hold this ton," but I know that yer'll be wanting more. After all, I'm not a charity. Now, this brings me onto my next point.'

I knew what was coming.

'Why don't you do a shift for me tonight, eh?'

I began to shake my head. I had known Tony for about a year, and he was forever asking me to do some work as a bouncer with him. He had an endless stream of work, night and day, working all over London, and was always on the lookout for help. The idea of working as a bouncer did not appeal to me at all. Why would I want to set myself up to get my head kicked in, or worse? And, if I had to defend myself – and I could, make no mistake about that – what if I ended up doing some guy a great deal of harm? I didn't fancy doing time because of it. No, that line of work was out, as far as I was concerned.

That was until Tony said the magic words: 'Double bubble Ian'. He grinned like Fagin, rubbing his fingers together. I was tempted.

'Double bubble, yer sure Tony?' I tried not to seem too interested, but we were talking about seventy quid here, something that I couldn't sniff at.

'I'm telling yer mate, seventy smackeroonies.'

We walked towards the car park where Tony's rust box of a car was parked. There were no lights in the little car park at the back of the gym. As Tony manoeuvred the car out to the road, my heart did a double somersault. I was scared that he would hit another car. Tony didn't seem too bothered. When he approached the main road, and just swung out into the path of a juggernaut, I thought my time was up! My life was definitely worth more than seventy quid, and I wasn't too happy about putting my trust in Tony. Because that is what I would have to do, if I decided to take on the job.

Tony was not one for giving up. We drove around the round-about at Bow, east London and headed for the bagel shop in Bethnal Green.

'Seventy quid could get yer some decent gear, and get yer set up for the next qualifier', he continued.

My need to succeed was very strong: I badly wanted to win. As soon as that thought dropped into my mind, without thinking any more about it, I told Tony I would do a shift.

'Yes, my son, yer've made the right move', he said with a lot of satisfaction in his voice.

We sat outside the bagel shop and demolished four salmon and cream cheese bagels, washing them down with a pint of cold milk.

By ten minutes to seven, Tony and I were just up the road from the venue for the night. The White Hart pub was a dilapidated establishment, which had seen better days. Tony had told me that he wanted to show me something, before we entered the pub. We walked round to the boot of his car. Tony fished around a bit. There was so much junk in his boot, it was a wonder he could find anything.

'Here grab a hold of this', he motioned.

'What's this for?' I looked in horror as he handed me a wooden baseball bat.

'This is called self-preservation', he replied.

'Nah, sorry mate, I can't handle this. It's asking for aggro.' I felt very uneasy, to say the least.

'Don't panic Ian. I guarantee yer, that we will have no trouble tonight. But, if a punter, starts to get a bit excited, one rap from this will sort 'im out.'

Reluctantly, I followed Tony into the pub. He spoke to the landlord, and I just nodded to him. We then took up our posts, just outside the door. I had shoved the baseball bat in the inside pocket of my leather jacket. Having it so close to my skin, was not reassuring. A quick glance at my watch told me that it was only 7.20 p.m. The night was still very, very young. The cold night air penetrated right through my clothing. It felt as though my body was seizing-up. I shoved my hands deeper into my jacket pockets. Wrong move, my knuckles touched the baseball bat. My hand recoiled out of my pocket and I decided to keep them both behind my back. As the people began to come in, I wished, increasingly, that I'd stayed at home. Everyone looked as though they belonged to the land of giants: even the women looked tall and threatening. And talk about mouthy! The ladies were so aggressive. Entry to the pub that night was by ticket only, and that's what caused a lot of the problems.

'Sorry love – no ticket – you can't come in.' I would say politely.

'Yer what?' a blonde wailing banshee shrieked back at me. 'I come 'ere every night, and you,' she pointed menacingly into my face, 'are not going to tell me otherwise.' She began to push against me, and the rest of her mates followed suit. This was hard for me, because I had never hit a woman, but this one was asking for it.

'Listen love, I said you can't come in.'

She wasn't having any of it. The pushing and shoving continued. Then a voice behind said, 'It's alright Ian, she's sweet, let her in'. The group of women pushed past me, tutting and muttering. 'Ere Tony, where did yer get him from, a bit too full of himself if yer ask me.'

'He's new love, he's new', Tony responded.

I felt a complete fool. If Tony had told me once, he told me a hundred times, admission by ticket only. I was only trying to do my job, and he overruled me. It was like that for the next few hours, I would say no, they couldn't come in without a ticket, and

Tony would overrule me and let them in. The trouble was, for the majority of people, the pub was their regular haunt: they spent most nights having a drink there. Now, that it was Christmas Eve, and tickets were required to get in, they felt that it was out of order. It was their local and that was that.

All this aggravation didn't do a lot for my self-confidence. I must've looked, to the punters, like someone who could handle himself: and anyone else if need be. The truth of the matter was, I was more than a little apprehensive. There was a strong underlying feeling of fear that I had to suppress continually. There were so many 'what ifs' running through my brain: What if someone pulls a knife out on me? What if a fight breaks out? Would I run, or would I steam in? What if the 'Old Bill' catches me with this bat?

Now and again my teeth would chatter, and my body would shake. I didn't know whether it was because of the cold weather or fear. I looked over at Tony and he was involved in conversation with a few guys. He was laughing and joking with them. That was another concerned I had – could I rely on him if it 'went off'? I was soon able to put that to the test.

By now it was 11.30 p.m. One more hour: it couldn't pass quickly enough for me. Tony had told me a while ago that he was going to check the toilets. He seemed to be gone a long time. Stamping my feet and beating my hands together to keep my circulation going, I glanced over my shoulder and was horrified to see my worst nightmare coming true. In the centre of the pub, a group had gathered – something was going off. I didn't know what to do – where was Tony?

A man pulled the door open and said to me, 'You're needed over there mate, looks like a bit of trouble'. Reluctantly, I waded my way through the sea of unyielding bodies. I stopped at the edge of the circle.

'Get off me yer dirty old man,' screamed a plump black woman.

'Yu is my gal tonight,' slurred an old black man.

'Help me somebody,' the woman pleaded.

Taking a deep breath, I sized up the situation. The old guy was molesting the woman. He was short and skinny – I could handle him, I thought. I straightened myself up, and marched up to the man, and got him in a bear hug. He didn't know what had hit him. With my strong arms restraining him, he didn't have a chance to break free. I pushed through the crowd, half carrying the man. I used the man's body as a battering ram to get through the door. The door flew open and I dropped him. He stumbled, and fell on the floor.

'Now, clear off home' I shouted at him. It felt good that I had managed to deal with the guy on my own. That feeling was short lived. The guy was well and truly angry. He began to cuss and shout, gesticulating wildly. I was cool and calm, until the man came close to me and, from nowhere it seemed, he pulled a knife out and waved it under my nose. The blade looked like it was ten foot long. I didn't have time to think clearly. Automatically, I pulled out the baseball bat, and whacked the man across the face. He fell in a crumpled heap to the floor. I pounced on him and stood on the hand that held the knife. I must've broken his hand, as he cried out in pain. Picking up the knife, I could see that it wasn't very big after all. I had quickly put the bat back, which was just as well, as two policemen appeared from out of the dark night, and collared me. I had trouble explaining the situation to them. I don't think that they believed me at first, but when they saw the knife, they let me go. They scraped the guy off the floor and flung him in the back of their 'meat wagon', then drove off.

'What's happening man?' asked Tony slapping me on the back.

'What's happening man?!' I shouted at him. 'Did you see that geezer with a blade, I nearly got stabbed man. Where were yer.' I was well upset.

'Well what happened?'

I filled him in.

'So what's your problem eh, good thing you had the bat then,' he grinned.

I didn't even bother responding to him. Every worry that I had had about being a bouncer had come true that night. It just confirmed to me that this was going to be the first and the last time for me. Or so I thought.

Early January was cold and frosty. The seventy quid was burning a hole in my pocket and I was eager to buy some steroids. The only drawback was Tony. After the fiasco at the pub, I wasn't keen to buy any gear from him. If he was unreliable at the job, how could I trust him to be my supplier? The problem of how I was going to get some gear was worrying me. It wasn't as though I could go into Boots and ask for it over the counter. I racked my brains to think of any people I knew who were into body building and whom I could trust, who might be able to help me, and came up with no-one. Then, one night, after work I was coming home on the bus, when some guy came upstairs, where I was sitting, and sat across the aisle to me. At the same time, we looked at each other, and realised that we knew each other.

'Ian, alright mate?'

'Sam, how are yer?'

Sam had been my first training partner. Boxing had been the thing that had got me into a gym, when I was fourteen. Coming from Forest Gate and Ilford, in east London, I would travel all the way to Dagenham Boys' Club to train as a boxer. I was inspired by *Rocky*, the movie, and I thought that I could give Sylvester Stallone a run for his money. From the time I started weight training, to help develop strength for boxing, I began to lose interest in the sport, and major more on developing my body. It was a wonderful thing to see my muscles blow up, and curve and shape, causing my body to look good.

My mum was amused by it all, 'Look at the state of your body. You look like the Michelin man.'

She would walk around the room, pretending to be me, pulling faces. This was particularly funny because Mum had long blonde hair and model-like looks. My older brother thought I was a bit of a nutcase and took no notice of me. Jason, my younger brother looked up to me, and even started doing some weights himself. Sadly, my Dad was not around. The last time I had heard from him was when I was about six. He had emigrated to Australia, and had sent me a Boomerang!

'So where are yer training now, Ian?' Sam asked.

'I'm still down at Allan's.'

Sam laughed: he knew what Allan was like. 'He hasn't changed then?'

'Not much,' I replied.

'How's Tony, is he still selling the gear?'

This was a great opener for me. I had been wondering how I could broach the subject of steroids, but hadn't come up with anything. But, as Sam had come right out with it himself, I launched straight in with 'I think he's still dealing, but, eh, do you still sell a bit yourself?'

'Yeah, why – you interested?'

I told him that I was.

'The only thing is, I don't know how to inject myself.'

Sam nodded his head at me and said 'No problem mate. Look, I'll sort you out. Everything you need, I can supply.'

He pulled a piece of paper and a stubby pencil out of his jacket pocket and wrote something down. He handed the paper to me.

'This is my number Ian. Give us a bell, say,' he pondered for a moment 'say in a couple of days, and I'll get it sorted for you.' I was well pleased.

It was a good thing I looked up, otherwise I would have missed my stop. Walking down the road, I thought that I was very lucky to have met up with Sam. Now my life could go in the direction that I wanted it to. I had seen the results of steroids, and I was confident that this was the way forward for me.

For the next couple of days, I poured over the pages of *Beef It* and *Arnold's Education of Body Builders* magazines. I wanted to emulate the guys I saw in the photos. Their gleaming, well-honed muscles were what I hankered after. I knew that once I started injecting, my body would soon look like theirs.

Sam didn't live too far from me, and we had arranged to meet in the chippy. We joked and laughed from the time we met, until we entered his house. His Mum was in. I said hello to her, then Sam quickly took me upstairs into his bedroom. We quickly demolished the saveloy and chips and washed it down with a can of coke. By now, I was feeling a bit uncomfortable. I have never been too fond of needles, especially knowing that one was going to be stuck into me. But, I was impressed with the way that Sam carried out the operation. First, he washed his hands. Then, he took out the syringe and needle from their sterile packs. He stuck the needle into the bottle, and drew up the liquid. Once the syringe barrel was full, he flicked the barrel to dispel all the air bubbles. He told me that he had to get rid of all the bubbles, otherwise, if he injected them into my body, I could end up with a heart attack, a stroke, or even dead. I was very nervous. It wouldn't have taken much for me to tell him to forget the whole thing. But, I knew I had to go through with it if wanted to achieve my dream.

'Now hold still Ian,' said Sam. I was jittery. I wasn't keen on having a needle stuck into me. With my hands on the back of a chair, I gripped tightly. Sam was giving me a lecture.

'I've got to stick the needle in the right place Ian. You see this muscle here,' he pointed to the top part of my bottom, 'very close to it is the sciatic nerve. One wrong jab and you're history, mate. You'll spend the rest of your days looking at life from a wheelchair, getting a disabled pension,' he grinned.

My knees buckled with fear. Sam had instructed me to place one leg behind the other so that the muscle to be injected was relaxed. I felt so weak, I wanted to sit down.

Clenching my teeth, I said, 'Just do it Sam, just do it!' He did. Immediately afterwards, I sat on the chair. I felt drained: not because of the effect of the injection, but because of the whole scenario leading up to it. It wasn't long before I started to feel myself again.

'Right,' said Sam, 'see you in a couple of days for the next lot.' I thanked him and went home.

By the third time, I was injecting myself. I really didn't want to, but I knew that I had to if I wanted to achieve my goal. Sam taught me stage by stage, how to correctly draw up the liquid in the syringe and aim the needle. It wasn't as bad as I thought it would be. Once I had done it, I knew that it wasn't going to be too hard. It took a couple of weeks to work, but it increased my body weight and strength.

Throughout the following twelve weeks, I was offered a couple of odd shifts doing some door work. Again, initially, I was reluctant, but the lure of £45 in my hand was enough to persuade me to take it. I worked in a club in Woolwich called the Flamingo. I had to wear formal dress: dicky-bow, white shirt and dinner jacket (bought cheap in an Oxfam shop). The job was a lot easier than my previous stint.

The downside of steroid-taking for me was losing my peace of mind. I had heard so many horror stories of people taking steroids and having massive heart attacks, liver or kidney failure, or just dropping dead, that I was frightened that it would happen to me: I couldn't relax. But, I continued to take them.

The twelve-week course was soon up and I had a break of four weeks. I was training twice a day, seven days a week. I recuperated so quickly from each workout that I was able to train frequently.

The British Body Building Championships were to be held in November 1986 and the qualifiers were monthly until then. I had decided to compete in the October trials, which meant that I needed to be taking another course of steroids as soon as possible.

My confidence was increasing. Not only was I feeling very happy with the way my body was taking shape, but other people's comments made me feel good.

'Ian, c'mon take your tee-shirt off and show the boys what you look like,' said Wag proudly. Wag was the owner of the gym I used to go to when I was younger. I had visited that day to do a bit of training. The compliments that the boys paid me made my ego swell.

The only cloud on the horizon was lack of money. A guy who trained in the gym in Bow, told me that the Ilford Palais was in need of doormen. I thought about it for a bit and realised that it was the only way for me to earn quick, easy money. So I went to see Joe the head doorman at the Palais, who gave me a job. The pay wasn't great, only thirty quid, but I couldn't afford to turn it down. I told Joe about the job I did in Woolwich.

'Sorry mate, there's no way that I can match £45: £30, top whack.'

I wasn't too happy, but said to Joe, 'Okay then, if you can give me five nights, I'll do it.'

He agreed.

My girlfriend Val, who was the sister of my mate Marcus, was not happy. As we were walking down the road she let rip.

'What do you mean you're gonna do five nights a week. What about me?' she shouted. 'All this relationship consists of is you, you, you. You're in the gym in the day, and now, you're going to be at the Palais at night. What is the point of us dating, eh Ian, what is the point?' Val was very angry – I knew I had to choose my words carefully.

'Well, the thing is Val, I am thinking about you. I'm doing this for us. Just think, when I'm a pro, and I'm on top, I'll be earning big bucks. You will never want for anything. You can shop 'till you drop then.'

She was quiet for a bit, then she answered, 'We'll see!'

The truth of the matter was, I was obsessed with body building and winning. I was obsessed with myself. Having a girlfriend was high on my list of priorities, but the number one spot belonged to me. Now I was in a position to go as far as I could go, I was determined to not only be good, but to be the best.

Chapter 2

JAMAICA

'Quick, upstairs in the bar,' shouted Joe.

The panic button had sounded, there must've been some trouble. Tearing through the reception area, I braced myself for what lay ahead. Bashing into the double doors, which swung open, I turned left and bounded up the staircase. There was no time to be polite and ask the punters to clear the way; my elbows spoke for me.

'Out the way, out the way,' I shouted at the startled people, who were spilling their drinks and choking on their cigarettes.

Already a couple of weeks had gone by, and I had more or less settled into my new job. It was funny how quickly, I had become acclimatised to the environment of the Palais. Initially, it was the lure of the money that had made me take the job of doorman in the first place. I just thought that I would have to grit my teeth, and bear it. But soon, I found myself quite liking the job, and all that went with it – even the violence.

I soon spotted the problem. A semicircle of people had gathered near to the bar. In the middle, there was some violent activity going on. As I got closer, I heard a blood-curdling scream: 'Get your hands off me'.

By now, there were quite a few other doormen who had also responded to the call. Two girls were bent low. Each girl was trying to tear out the roots of the other's hair. It was awful. The fact that two women were fighting was bad enough, but it was the way they were mauling each other that seemed so terrible. I charged in, and grabbed the girl nearest to me. Tugging her away from her opponent wasn't easy. To make matters worse, the other girl had a gang of mates with her, who were just as ferocious and hungry for blood as she was. Yanking them apart took all my strength. I held onto the girl around the waist. My plan was to get her as far away from the scene as possible. Her enemies had other ideas. They encircled both the girl myself, and began to attack both of us.

'Let me get her.'

'I'm gonna kill you.'

A leg seemed to swing from out of nowhere. A very high-heeled shoe was attached to it. The foot caught the girl I was holding, fully in the face, connecting with her nose. Blood began to gush out, like a waterfall. The sight of blood seemed to incite the pack of girls, who were like baying wolves. Even as I was half carrying, half dragging the girl down the stairs, these crazy girls were still attacking us. A high-heeled shoe was repeatedly being hammered into my back – and it hurt – but there wasn't anything that I could do.

I eventually managed to get her into the ladies' loo. She was hysterical. The poor girl was covered in blood – her hair, her clothes, everything. She tried to clean herself up. Meanwhile, I had to lean against the door, as the other girls were still trying to get to her. They were kicking the door, trying to get in. Finally, when the other doorman had got rid of them, I brought the girl out, got her in a cab, and off she went. What a shift!

Later that night, at home, as I cleaned the blood off my clothes, I wondered if it was all worth it. Yes, I needed the money badly, but perhaps there was another way of earning it.

My body ached from the punches and kicks I had received from the girls. I was sore all over. Sometimes, I wished that I had been born with some sort of talent, like an artist, for instance. I would have loved to have become a professional footballer. That way, I could have pursued my dream of being 'somebody', without having to have artificial help. That was my true aim. The thought of living my whole life as a 'nobody' was depressing. I had to achieve something with my life. That was the whole point. It was my life, and if I didn't make good use of it, who would? Those thoughts continually recurred in my mind. I had to do better. I had to win.

The seeds of this obsessive mindset were first sown when I lived in Jamaica. Tom, my step-father, was a vet. He married my Mum when I was about five or six years old. Tom's temper was well-known throughout the family. Profanity was his middle name! For years, I assumed that swearing was a normal part of life. Whenever my mum and Tom started a fight, we children knew it was time to disappear. Wild accusations, would precede name calling. Slaps and punches would follow soon after. Most of the fisticuffs would come from Mum. She was a formidable antagonist. Mum gave Tom as good as she got – and more! When we heard the front door slam, we knew that Tom had run out, and it was safe for us to come back.

Mum and Tom's relationship was precarious. There was no love in it, as far as I could see. Mum seemed to have no positive feelings for Tom and, from his behaviour, it seemed as though he had little love for Mum. But, this was how it appeared from my viewpoint, as a child. Couples who are violent to one another, can still love each other – but at that time, it seemed like a relationship filled with hatred.

My own relationship with Tom was like having two strangers, living in the same house. He, as far as I can remember, never cuddled, or kissed me, or showed any affection towards me. My two half-brothers (who were like full brothers to me) didn't fare any better with him. My heart was like a block of ice, whenever I thought of Tom. His was probably the same, judging by his attitude towards me.

'You're as thick, as two short planks, you'll never amount to anything.'

These words revolved around in my mind for years, and I was convinced that I would end up as a professional dustman! Jamaica changed all that.

Mum and Tom's relationship had all but dissolved. For a number of years they had, by mutual agreement, lived apart, although they still kept in contact with each other because of the children.

The Christmas that I was twelve, my Mum bought us some strange presents: a snorkel, swimming goggles and flippers. My sister, brothers and I were puzzled. Then my Mum dropped a bombshell: 'Get packed kids, we're all off to live in Jamaica'.

There wasn't enough time to take in all that it would entail. I kept thinking about not seeing my normal habitat and missing all my friends, although it was a wonderful feeling telling my teachers that I wouldn't be in school any longer, as I was emigrating to Jamaica. The downside was, not being able to play for the school football team.

Jamaica. Stepping off the plane at Montego Bay into 70 °F was bliss. We had left England covered in snow. I knew, from my first few steps on Jamaican soil, that I was going to love it – and I did.

I was meant to go to high school, but for some reason it never materialised. So, for a whole year, I didn't go to school at all. My education came through the experiences of life I gained during that year. I explored the island from coast to coast. We lived near Ocho Rios, which is famous because of Dunn's River waterfalls. I spent many of my days fishing and swimming. Some days were spent going up into the mountains with friends. Every day was long and lazy.

Everyone had a machete, including me. It wasn't for violent purposes, just for everyday use: chopping down the bush as I went on my walkabouts; cutting open jelly coconuts so I could drink the juice. It made me feel grown up, carrying a machete every day.

I didn't cut my hair, for the whole year. It grew long, and the sun bleached it blonde. The local girls thought I was a novelty, and showed great interest in me. I was living out many people's fantasy.

'Hey bwoy, come 'ere' a total stranger would shout in the street. The normal response was to shout back.

Bob Marley was mega popular, and wherever I went I would be sure to hear one of his songs being played. Music features greatly in Jamaican culture and stereo speakers were played the loudest I had ever heard.

The food was fantastic: jerk chicken or pork, ackee and salt fish, rice and peas, Jamaican patties, hard dough bread, buns and cheese.

To me, everything about Jamaica was great. Jamaica altered my mindset. It made me realise that there was more to life than I had been experiencing, and affected my future expectations, which had, until then, been very limited indeed.

Yes, in Jamaica I grew taller, my hair grew longer and my skin became darker. I spent my days on the beach, and my nights drinking Red Stripe beer. I knew that this wasn't 'real life', yet the experience opened up parts of my mind, that would have other-wise remained closed. Whilst my school friends in England would be talking about becoming a plumber's mate or a mechanic, I had made up my mind that I was going to be 'somebody'!

Life after Jamaica was very depressing. Driving through the streets of London, from Heathrow Airport was a downer. Every-where was grey: grey skies; grey buildings; grey atmosphere. Even the people looked grey. It didn't take long for my mind to be re-filled with grey images.

School was a nightmare. I hadn't been the best pupil before, but now, after my Caribbean experience, I just couldn't settle in. My old school, Wanstead High was full and, therefore, I had to go to another school. The nearest one was Fairlop Waters, which was two bus-rides away.

From the first day, I had problems. Being a teenager isn't easy: the pressures of life seem to intensify, making simple things complicated. Depression wrapped itself around me like a second skin. This went with me everywhere I went. I hated going to lessons and it wasn't long before I started to have run-ins with the teachers. When I really went over the top, I was suspended. Once back on school turf, I would pick up where I had left off. To say I was a nuisance was an understatement.

I made a few friends in my new school. These boys were of a similar calibre to me. We were the school bullies. It was not unusual for us to approach another boy and start fighting with him for no reason. Thumping someone for their dinner money was an everyday occurrence! In fact, my gang and I had a little racket going. We actually had a book with names, days and amounts that were due. If anyone decided not to pay up (which they never did) we would sort them out. One boy was so terrified of us that he didn't come to school for a few weeks. When he finally did, his mother came too. I was summoned to the Head's office. Being a bit cocky, I wasn't too bothered about seeing the Headmaster. At first, he told me what the boy had claimed, and then he gave me room to tell my side of the story. I spun him some yarn about not having enough money to get home from school, because I had to change buses, and how I come from a big family, and anything else that flashed through my brain that sounded good. He not only believed my web of half-lies, but he said, 'Ian, in the future if you have any more difficulties, please come and see me'. What a joke!

As time went on, I hardly attended lessons, I could see no reason to go. I wasn't learning anything – there seemed no point. I slid comfortably into truancy. Once we had got our quota of dinner money for the day, my mates and I would take off to Pic-a-Pet, a pet shop just off the high street. At the back of the shop was an amusement arcade, with fruit machines, Space Invaders and pool tables, which attracted young boys in similar situations – school 'bunkers' and general lowlife. The smoky atmosphere was conducive to all manner of illegalities. By the time I reached fifteen, it seemed like a waste of time even attempting to go to school – so I left. All day, every day was spent playing pool and arcade games.

At home, post-Jamaica was having an effect too. Mum and Tom's relationship was virtually over. What finally pushed it over the edge was a woman called Pauline turning up on our doorstep. She was Tom's 'other woman'. Tom had started dating her in Jamaica. She was a professional limbo dancer: as bendy as a piece of foam! I think that might have been one of the things that attracted Tom to her in the first place.

Pauline was a demanding woman. In her lilting West Indian accent she said to Mum, 'Yu have to all move out. I's come to take over yur house.'

After the initial shock, Mum snapped into action. She drew back her arm, balled her hand into a fist, and whacked Pauline in the mouth. The blow caused Pauline to fall back down the path. Mum shut the door. Nothing more had to be said. It was a while before Tom showed his face in our house again.

I still had contact with Tom. At 16, I had no qualifications, or any prospect of earning money. I knew that Tom had a lot of customers who avoided paying him, so I offered him my services as a debt collector. I started work right away. My natural ability brought me attention. Stan was a debt collector, but on a far superior scale to myself. He asked me if I wanted to earn some serious money. How could I resist! For forty pounds a day, I would accompany him on his travels around London. He would leave his van, to pay a visit and often returned to the van carrying bundles of money. Whoever it was, paid up. My job was to wait in the van with a huge baseball bat. If anything went off, I was meant to rush over to Stan's aid, and wield the bat across heads. It never happened, because Stan was a very persuasive man. I was glad that my services weren't called upon as, to be perfectly honest, I was a bit nervous – in fact I wasn't sure if I had enough guts to go out there and help him!

* * *

I soon realised that to continue working at the Ilford Palais – and survive, I would need some tools of the trade. I purchased a knuckle-duster. It was a strip of heavy metal that sat across the knuckles of my right hand. It was a good investment – I was never without it.

Most nights at the Palais, six or seven fights would go off. Monday nights were the worst. This was the night for the over twenty-fives, and we all knew it. One Monday night, after a very eventful shift I was glad to be going home. Ron, the other guy who was doing the shift with me, didn't live too far from where I was staying. At 3 a.m. there were no buses running and, as Ron didn't have any wheels, I would usually drop him home.

This particular night, we were driving along, chatting, when I noticed a car with glaring lights, driving close to my bumper. It wasn't long before I realised that the car behind was following us. It eventually drew alongside, and then overtook us. As the car passed, I recognised the men. Earlier at the Palais, Ron and I had had to throw them out, as they were acting up. They spent the remainder of our shift, driving up and down, past the Palais, pretending that their hands were guns, and that they were shooting us.

The car slowed to a halt, right in front of us. I stopped my car.

'What we gonna do Ian?' asked Ron.

There was no doubt in my mind what I was going to do.

'We're gonna get 'em, now.'

It really annoyed me that somebody had the nerve to follow me home. It was an out and out liberty. I leapt out of the car like Superman, and made a beeline for their car. I don't think that they knew what hit them. As I got to the driver's side of the car, the driver was just getting out. I grabbed the door as he stood up. My immediate reaction was to squash him in the door. I wasn't sure if he had a gun or some other deadly implement and I wasn't going to give him a chance to use it. I began to pound on his face with my knuckle-duster clad hand. I wanted to rearrange his features. He screamed out in pain, but after a while, he went silent: I had knocked him unconscious. I was holding him up, but as soon as I let the door go, he flopped down onto the floor. There was blood everywhere.

Meanwhile, Ron had wrenched the heavy screwdriver out of the other guy's hand, and was using it on him. This guy was still in the car, and he was taking a heavy battering.

'Ron, Ron, stop. That's enough let's go', I shouted. I could see that if I had left Ron to his own devices, he could have killed the guy.

We drove off. I didn't take Ron straight home, but did a few detours, just in case we were being followed. We weren't. By the time I dropped Ron off, we were laughing about the night's events. Those guys had thought they were going to teach us a lesson but, in fact, it was they who were taught one!

Later that night, as I was eating a bowl of cornflakes, Dean, the assistant manager of the Palais called me. The two guys Ron and I had sorted out had been picked up by the Police. They told the Police that two doormen at the Ilford Palais were responsible. The Police went straight to the Palais with the guys, who picked out Dean as the perpetrator of the crime. The Police arrested him, but had to finally let him go. Dean was short and weighed about 9 stone. Physically, it would have been impossible for him to have inflicted their injuries. I laughed even more. It was amusing.

The money was now rolling in from my door work. I was again taking steroids and I now needed to diet seriously if I wanted to win. I also heard that an old training partner of mine, who was now a competitor, was using seventeen or eighteen different types of steroids. I was only taking two or three, so I decided to purchase more. Someone told me of a veterinary drug which was supposed to be a powerful drug to use. At that time, I was living above Tom's surgery in the small, one-bedroom flat.

(When I was seventeen, going on eighteen, my Mum decided to up and leave London, and head for the sunny shores of Clacton-on-Sea. Life outside London was incomprehensible to me. So, I stayed on alone in our empty house in Ilford for about six months without electricity, gas, water or a phone – nothing. I slept on a mattress on the floorboards, with a carving knife under my pillow. When I was at the gym, I was able to shower there, and use the microwave for cooking. I also supported myself by doing a bit of work for Tom, who felt sorry for me and offered me the flat. That's how I became Tom's tenant.)

I repaid Tom for his generosity by nipping down from the flat, and helping myself from his store of drugs. I found a bottle of the substance: on the label it read, 'Dosage: horses – 1 ml per week; bovine – 0.5 ml per week. I started injecting 2 ml per day! The results were noticeable quickly. I ignored the fact that the label clearly stated that it wasn't to be adminstered to humans. These steroids were going to help me win.

The combination of the steroids and the rationing of food was getting to me: I was getting increasingly aggressive.

Chapter 3

TOP TOUCH

I was psyched up to the max. My determination to win the championships was high. My body had never looked so good: the dieting and training had really paid off. On the day of the championships, I was feeling confident, and very positive.

At the weigh-in, I gave the other competitors the 'once over'. Comparing them to myself, I was confident that I was better. Some of my friends from the gym had accompanied me to the competition. They agreed with me that, not only was I looking good but, if they were the judges, they wouldn't hesitate in picking me as the winner.

In the pre-judging section of the championships I did well, and I was confident that I would win. But I didn't. I was freaked out. I came second, which just wasn't good enough for me. The winner was a guy who had won previous championships, and I think that the judges were swayed by a 'name' – well that's my story.

Here I was, a year on from my last competition, tanked up to the hilt on steroids, and still I attained the same position. My friends' words of comfort: 'You were robbed Ian, you were robbed', did not pacify me. I wanted to win, and anything less was of no interest to me. I was so fed-up: nothing seemed to be going my way, even though I was putting so much into it. I considered quitting.

Such thoughts rolled around my mind like a marble on a ship's deck. After much soul-searching, I decided to give it another shot. I couldn't give up now, as I didn't know what else I could do. I felt as though I had backed myself into a corner, and there was only one course of action that I could take. I had big plans for myself, and I knew that the only person that could carry them out was ME.

I had been dating Valerie, for a couple of years. She was a patient, long-suffering girl. To add to my concerns, Valerie started to press me about our relationship. I loved Val, but I was totally wrapped up in my body building and the prestige and success that winning would bring. The main problem with our relationship was me. I was totally, and utterly concerned with myself. Most of the money that I earned was spent on the essentials of living and drugs. Body building is an expensive business. Food is a high priority: a chicken a day, lots of eggs, lots of vegetables, and fresh and tinned fish. Food supplements cost me a bomb – amino acids, liver tablets, protein and carbohydrate drinks – the list was endless.

Valerie knew that I loved her, and she, rightly, wanted more commitment from me. We decided, after Christmas 1987, to think seriously about where our relationship was going. We arranged to have a meal in Chinatown, a restaurant in Ilford, to discuss this. For the previous two weeks I had been taking a new steroid which was very, very strong, and toxic. It came in 50 mg tablets. By taking one a day, I immediately noticed the difference. My strength and weight increased quickly. Sam, my supplier advised me that one would not be enough. He told me that four a day was what I should be on.

'Just look at me, Ian', he said.

I had to admit that Sam looked in fine form, but that would mean that I was taking fourteen tablets and an injectable every day.

Unfortunately, I took the four tablets on the day that Valerie and I were to have our 'in-depth' conversation about our relationship. Throughout the day, I had been getting cramps and stomach pains, but I had ignored them. When the meal was served up, I was in severe pain, but I was trying to hold it together. Not wanting to let Val see that I was in a bad way, I gritted my teeth. I told her that we should get married. I had toyed with the idea of getting married, but thought that it would make more sense if we just lived together. But with the pain raging in my guts, I needed to curtail the conversation.

'Married – you sure Ian?'

'Yeah, yeah Val. Look, I love you, you love me, let's just do it.'

'When,' said Valerie, a bit shocked.

'Soon, a couple of weeks time.'

Slightly dazed, Val replied, 'What about arrangements, like where, and who's coming. And how much is it going to cost?'

The pain was intensifying.

'Don't worry, we can borrow some money off my Mum, and maybe your Dad. Lets just get the ball rolling, it will sort itself out.'

I wanted to cut the talk and just go home. But the pain was so bad, I had to excuse myself and go to the loo.

I was drenched in sweat. The loos were conveniently empty. I threw myself onto the tiled floor, and unbuttoned my jeans. That was it. The pain was so great, that I couldn't do any more. My kidneys felt as though they had been kicked with hobnail boots. My whole body felt violated. It felt as though death was around the corner. This was it: at the tender age of twenty-one, my life was over. All those plans of getting married were for nothing – I wouldn't be there! Lying sprawled out on the floor, I breathed deeply and wondered how Sam was able to take all those pills and live to tell the tale?

Fifteen minutes later, the pain had subsided. Slowly, I eased myself up, buttoned my jeans and went back out to Val.

'Where have you been?' she asked.

'Oh, I had a bit of a stomach ache.' I played down my trauma. I didn't want Valerie to know what I had been up to. I only wanted her to see the good side of me.

The wedding day was set. We were married in Valerie's parents' church on 16 January 1988. Our honeymoon was spent in a hotel in Clacton. Within two days, I was in the hotel gym, working-out. Valerie was shocked and disappointed that, on our honeymoon, I preferred spend time in the gym, to spending the whole time with her.

This is how the early years of our marriage were. I saw more of the inside of gyms than I did our flat. It was a constant bone of contention between us. Valerie began to get on my case about earning 'proper' money – getting a job, but I didn't want to know. A regular job would not bring me what I was yearning for. I tried to reason with Valerie about my goals and ambitions, but she was having none of it. I was afraid of losing her, so I agreed to apply for a job as a Fireman. I didn't get the job, which I was relieved about, but it brought home to me the seriousness of being a husband: it was loaded with responsibilities.

I worked out even harder. My need to win was growing by the minute. I now had to prove to Valerie that training was a valid occupation. I was pumping iron twice a day.

The need to get more money was paramount. Sam introduced me to a guy who was a well-known supplier. I decided to go into partnership with him, but it didn't last. I then started dealing on my own. I was earning good money, but never let on to Valerie how much was slipping through my fingers. As the money was coming in, I was swallowing or injecting it away.

Around this time I was offered a job at Top Touch, a club in Dagenham. I took the job because its rate of pay was better than I was getting at the Palais. I was working with older guys, which I preferred. I was impressed with the way these guys presented themselves for work, in dinner suits and ties, and they took a pride in their work. I felt as though I had taken a step up in life. The other benefit for me in working at the club was that I was able to increase my clientele. There was a gym at the end of the road. Most of the members came to the club after working-out. Some of the guys were really mouthy and flash. Working on the front door, we had to put up with a lot of nonsense. There was one particular guy who, when we got chatting, asked if I knew anyone who could get hold of some gear. I told him that I could sort him out with some stuff and he became one of my regular punters for injectables. I didn't like this guy. He irritated me, and bored me with his incessant chatting. He was too frightened to inject himself, so rather sheepishly asked me if I could do it. He didn't realise it, but whilst he was babbling on about a load of rubbish, I was injecting him with an empty syringe barrel. After he paid me about a hundred quid, I would inject him, and send him on his way. He was happy, but in reality, he wasn't getting anything. I used the drug on myself!

Top Touch was known as a nightclub, but in reality it was a drinking man's club. Many of the punters were in their early thirties and beyond. Most of the time things were peaceful, but when something went off, it was a big affair.

Barry and Gary, who worked with me at Top Touch, were twins. They reminded me of the Krays, in that they were not the sort of people that you would mess with: they could handle themselves. One night Barry came down to the front door, and said, 'Listen guys, I think that something's gonna go off tonight. There's a large crowd of 'townies' upstairs, and I know that they are gonna be up for it.' He didn't have to say any more. Chris, the other guy on the door, and I knew what would be expected of us. My heart did a few flips. Excitement and fear, mingled with the rush of adrenaline, flooded my blood stream. I slipped my hand into my pocket, and felt the cold metal of the knuckle-duster: it was reassuring. The baseball bat was resting inside my jacket pocket. I had pulled some of the stitching out to accommodate it. The 'fight and flight' mechanism kicked in. I was ready to go to war. Five minutes later, we were still downstairs, limbering up ready for the call. It came.

Simon, who was Barry's stepson, worked the cloakroom. He

shouted down to us: 'Ian, Chris, quick, it's going off.'

Without more ado, we bounded up the stairs, taking them two at a time. Bursting in through the double doors, we saw a commotion around the bar area. Steaming through the dancing crowds, we approached the trouble. It was obvious that someone had taken a beating. One guy had blood coming out of his nose. Barry was holding him back, while Gary was held onto his opponent. There were groups of men surrounding them. It looked as though Barry and Gary had, once again, sorted out the business. A stab of disappointment punctured my enthusiasm. I had been looking forward to a good old punch-up.

Since I had started working at Top Touch, I felt that I had to prove myself to the guys. It wasn't anything they said, or indicated in their attitude towards me. Perhaps it was because these guys were older and wiser than any other doormen that I had worked with, that I felt I needed to show them that I was on their level, and could handle anything that came up.

Later that night, I got my chance. My duster was securely fitted to my hand. That was a good job because, within a matter of seconds, some nutcase rushed out from the crowd, and crashed straight into Chris, socking him in the side of his face. The guy seemed to be no more than five foot tall. I grabbed him, and began to pound his head. He bent low, to ward off my blows, but I backed him against a pillar, and really gave it to him. Chris soon joined me, and while I was whacking him in the head, Chris was giving his stomach a good going over. The guy didn't stand a chance.

I began to enjoy myself. With every punch, I was warming to the job in hand. Suddenly, I felt a blow to my back. Turning round to see what was happening, I saw four or five guys bundle Chris, backing him into the bar. They started to lay into him. Then I realised that I too was being set up. A couple of guys on either side of me, were trying to hit me. As I grabbed hold of them, we all toppled to the floor. Fortunately, I fell on top of them. I managed to get to my feet. A missile of broken glass whizzed past my face. It became embedded into the wall opposite me. Heaving a sigh of relief, I turned and saw that virtually the whole nightclub had become a mass of fighting bodies. Chairs were being thrown everywhere. Glasses and bottles were flying through the air, hitting anything that was in their path. I couldn't see Chris, or Barry or Gary. I felt like I was on a desert island surrounded by sharks.

'Ian,' I thought to myself, 'you have got to come out of this in one piece.'

The guy who had launched the glass missile at me, was still standing quite close by. I grabbed him in a rugby tackle, and bundled him out, through the fighting mass and through the double doors. He was trying to resist me, but he wasn't strong enough. At the top of the stairs, he started screaming: he knew what was coming. Showing no mercy, and loving every minute of it, I pitched the man backwards down the stairs. He bounced and crashed his way to the bottom. Out of the corner of my eye, I saw the VIP lounge room being ransacked. The payphone was being pulled off the wall and someone was yanking the till off the bar. For a moment, I was at a loss as to what to do first. Simon helped me make a decision.

'Quick Ian, Barry's in trouble.'

I ran back through the doors, and saw at once that Barry had taken a bit of a beating. He was heaving himself up off the floor. His jacket had been ripped and blood was seeping from his face. A group of guys were still hovering around him, like predatory wolves. They wanted more blood. I ran over to Barry's aid. Gary came out of nowhere, and started to assess the situation.

'Right, that's it. It's over. Out. Everyone out.'

Taking a cue from him, I started to grab some of the troublemakers, herding them towards the door.

'Out, that's it, out.'

These guys were still a bit resistant, but now that there was a group of doormen ready to deal with more trouble, it was as though the wind had been taken out of their sails.

At the top of the stairs, we shoved them hard. They soon got the message. Outside the club, as they spewed through the doors, I noticed the coppers, sitting in their panda cars, passively looking on. Chris shouted to them sarcastically,

'Oi, you've been a great help, thanks!'

They sat looking at us as though we were aliens.

Back in the club it looked as if World War Three had taken place. The floor was a sea of broken glass. There wasn't a whole table or chair in sight. There were still about a hundred and fifty people in the club. Amazingly, the DJ still had the music belting out. This really wound Barry up. Making his way to the back of the club where the DJ had his spot, he shouted:

'Shut this music off. What's the matter with you, we've got to clear this place, and you still think it's party time!' Abruptly the music stopped. We cleared the place, then sat down to toast ourselves on the good job we had done. We were really pleased with ourselves, even though some of us had taken a bit of a battering, and were blood-stained and had ripped clothes.

The management finally came out from their hiding place – now that it was all over. They were pleased with our efforts to quell the aggro, but I could tell that having their livelihood smashed up, hadn't made them too happy.

Driving home, I was well pleased with myself. I felt that I had really proved something that night. Recounting in my mind the conversation that we had had after the fight, I felt smug and proud, as someone had noticed how I had thrown the guy down the stairs. It gave my ego a boost. I was glad that an opportunity had arisen for me to show these hard guys that I was up for it, and could handle myself, and I was eager for another chance to prove myself.

* * *

I had qualified for the British finals. I wanted 1989 to be a good year for me. If I won (which I was willing myself to do), it would be a step closer to getting a pro card, which would mean I could then compete professionally, and perhaps get sponsorship. It would also mean that I would at last be able to prove to Valerie, that body building was indeed a viable occupation, that had great benefits.

I continued to experiment with drugs. Now that I had crossed the line from drug-free to drug-filled, I was willing to put anything into my body, if it would help me to come first. I still listened to Sam about drugs: he knew a lot about them. He was the one who told me about another new 'wonder drug', which was injected straight into the bicep muscle and immediately made the muscle swell. It lasted for only twenty-four hours and needed to be administered two or three days before a competition. Sam gave me some, and I became a guinea pig. As Sam held the ampoule to me, he taunted me saying, 'Do you really think you can do this'.

'Yes,' I replied confidently.

It wasn't hard for me to say it. The desire to win was overwhelming. I did not want to ever lose again. Most body builders I knew, were taking steroids, but what I was about to inject into my body was something that, at the time, nobody else was using.

Back at home, I drew up the potion into the syringe, and injected it into my muscle. Instantly, before my eyes, my bicep increased in size. It was miraculous. Feeling very pleased with myself, I lay down on the settee to have forty winks.

The bell rang. It was my older brother Lloyd. He had come to see me, and to find out how my 'career' was progressing. I didn't want him to find out about my steroid-taking. Lloyd was very much against drugs, and he would have been disappointed if he had found out.

'C'mon then, let's see your body.'

I was pleased that I had just injected myself, and that Lloyd would be the first to see the results. Lifting up my tee-shirt, I preened myself in front of him. Smiling, he walked round me and said, 'Very nice, very nice'. Lifting my arms, I showed him my pumped-up biceps. He was shocked.

'What have you been doing?' he asked.

I was shocked myself. Since I had fallen asleep they had increased in size even more. Lying, I said to him, 'Yeah, yeah, I've been doing a lot of cable curls'.

He started to reassure me that this was the year for me, and that he was sure that I was going to become British Champion.

Chapter 4

KNOCK-BACK

Exhilarated – that's how I felt. The bright spotlights dazzled my eyes. The crowds were screaming and cheering. The MC for the evening was stirring the people up.

'C'mon,' he shouted, 'who's gonna win tonight?'

The crowd was shouting out the names of their favourites. I heard my name being called out. It was a boost to my already inflated ego. Air horns were tooting and music was blaring from the loud speakers around the hall. Baby oil and sweat mingled together on my skin. My muscles stood out, glistening like precious jewels. I was centre stage. In my heart I believed that I was already the winner. The trophy was right in front of me. In my mind, I could feel the cool metal in my hands as I held the trophy aloft, to the wild applause of the crowd. My heart was beating nineteen to the dozen. Clenching my fists, I wanted to jump up and down and shout out 'Yes, I've done it!' It was hard for me to contain myself.

The eyes of the judges continued to appraise each competitor. As the minutes ticked away, I was sure I was about to be announced as the winner.

'Alright folks,' boomed the MC, 'I have now been given the names of the winners.' A quietness fell on the crowd.

'In sixth place . . .'

The MC called the names of the competitors, until he got to first. I was holding something in my hands. I wasn't sure what it was, or how it got there. I stood there waiting.

'The 1989 British Body Building Middleweight Champion is Ian . . . McCready.'

The noise that erupted in the arena was deafening. I was in shock. Ian turned round to me, 'I thought you'd won,' he said.

Numbness enveloped my brain. It was hard for me to think straight. Maybe our surnames had got mixed up and it should have been McDowall not McCready.

All the competitors, including myself were herded backstage. Only the winners of the first three places were left on stage to soak up the mighty applause from the audience.

Backstage, my brain kicked into gear. Looking down at my hands, I saw that I had been given a trophy.

'I can't believe you came fifth Ian, something's wrong,' said one of the guys who had been on stage with me.

'Yeah man, you should've won,' everyone with me agreed. I should really have been on that stage receiving all that acclaim. I looked at my trophy. It sickened me to see the word 'fifth'. In disgust I flung it on the floor, and walked off. One of the competition officials came over to me and offered me my expenses. Pushing him away from me, I said angrily, 'I don't want that. What do I want with that. You've robbed me.' I stormed off.

In the changing room, my mind somersaulted back to an incident that had occurred a month earlier. I had been doing a stint at the Bow gym. There weren't many people around and I was drinking a protein drink and Tony was sitting chatting to me. A sales rep came in and began to take stuff out of his bag. He started giving us a sales spiel about his body building products, and how good they were. I started to take the mickey out of him. He was tall, skinny and bald. I wanted to know, how someone who looked as he did could promote the benefits of such products. Arrogantly, I said to him, 'Well, they haven't done anything for you mate!'

Tony, by now, was in stitches. That only encouraged me and I wouldn't let up. The guy didn't get a chance to give us a full display of his wares. In the end he packed up and went. Even as he walked through the door, I was giving him stick. He was well upset. I was so proud of my body, and all the work that I did to maintain my wonderful shape, that I couldn't take seriously some skinny guy, coming to my gym, and trying to sell me a load of rubbish.

'Hey Ian, do you know who he was?' asked Tony.

'Some skinny sales rep,' I laughed.

Grinning, Tony replied, 'He's one of the judges of the EFBB'.

'Who cares?' I didn't.

A month later, during the morning of the championships, after the first round, I got changed and was making my way across the arena with Sam, who was telling me that I was the biggest and the best, and that I was sure to win. Suddenly, a voice bellowed out behind me, 'Hey boy!' I didn't think he was talking to me, but nevertheless, I turned around and was surprised to see the 'skinny sales rep', in an official judge's blazer, with a badge saying that he was the head judge. I gulped. Speaking humbly, I pointed to myself and said 'Are you talking to me?'

Pointing his finger at me he said, 'You were chewing gum when you were on stage, weren't you?' He was surrounded by some of the other judges. The hairs on my arms stood up like soldiers to attention. I hadn't been chewing gum, but I sensed that this man was out to humiliate me. Responding to his question I assured him that I wasn't. The head judge straightened up his shoulders, and looked me straight in the eye. I could tell that he was loving every minute of it. This was his moment of power.

'Yes you were,' he sneered, 'and for that, we have deducted five points from your score.' He marched off.

I was upset and confused, but Sam told me not to worry, and that five points were so minor that they wouldn't make any difference overall. I wasn't so sure.

Now that I had been placed fifth, I realised that the judge had got his revenge and that with this guy as the head judge, I was never ever going to win an EFBB championship. I decided that the only thing to do was to change federations. I would now compete with the World Amateur Body Building Association (WABBA). There was no way that I was going to give up.

For months after my defeat, I couldn't get the fiasco out of my mind. My mood swung between rage, hatred and depression, but my determination did not falter. I wanted to be a winner.

At this time in my life nothing seemed to be going right. I trained and took more steroids, but they didn't help me to achieve a thing. I was consumed with myself: morning, noon and night, it was all I thought about. Valerie, and my new daughter, Bianca, didn't get a look in. Most of the money that I earned was spent on me. Valerie and I would have rows about money, and she was desperate for me to get a proper job. Doing a normal job was out of the question as far as I was concerned. I had made my mind up that I was going to continue with the body building, until I won, and nothing and no-one was going to stop me. My wife said that she needed money for nappies and other baby paraphernalia. I loved my wife and child, but I loved me more. I just couldn't part with much money: I needed it for me.

The arguments between Val and I were becoming more serious. We talked, or shouted, about going our separate ways, but living on my own again wasn't something I wanted to think seriously about. I didn't want to leave my baby girl. My Dad had left me, and I didn't want Bianca to go through the same pain and rejection as I did. But, at the same time, I had to do what I had to do.

We were living in a council flat on a big estate. My grey surroundings caused me to sink to lower depths of depression. I drove around in an old banger, that repeatedly broke down at the wrong time. Nothing was working out for me. Why?

Someone had once told me that a curse had been put on my life. At the time, I thought this was rubbish. I didn't believe in white or black witches. It was all nonsense. Curses were only words after all!

Five o'clock one morning, after walking in the rain for nearly an hour, I arrived home with my mood at rock bottom. My car had clapped out again, and I didn't have the money to fix it up, or even get a cab home. Laying on my bed, exhausted, my thoughts came back to the curse. It seemed so irrational and stupid. But, something was going on which I was powerless to change.

Money was one of my main problems. Like many people, I just didn't have enough. If Valerie had known how much dosh was slipping through my fingers to support my drug habit, she would have killed me. Consequently, I made sure she didn't find out!

I knew that my time at Top Touch was soon coming to an end. Since the big fight, the club owners just couldn't pull it back again. The punters were becoming fewer and fewer, and we doormen were in danger of losing our jobs. The long and the short of the situation was, I needed more work.

One of the doormen at a club I used to do a few daytime stints at, asked if I could do him a really big favour.

'Ere Ian, you busy tonight?'

'Why, what do you want?'

It was usual for us doormen to look after each other – just like family! Leaning close to me he whispered, 'Would you collect a shooter from Frank for me, and drop it up at Chimes tonight?'

'Yeah yeah, no problem Al, I'll do it for you.'

Chimes was a nightclub in north London. It was really just a pub with a late licence. It was renowned for trouble. When I got to Frank's that evening, he told me that he wasn't too happy about giving Al the gun.

'You know what Al is like, he's a class one nutter. I don't want him killing anyone, and then have the shooter traced back to me.'

I nodded my head in agreement, but there wasn't much I could say or do. It was entirely up to Frank, whether he let Al have his gun or not.

Outside Chimes that evening, I gave Al the nod. He quietly
slipped away from his post and followed me to the car park.
Opening the boot of my car, I pointed to the plastic bag that was
concealing the gun. Al slipped it under his coat, and half walked,
half ran back to the club, with me following, hot on his heels. He
went into the toilet to examine the piece, while I had a look around
the club. It was decorated nicely, as some nightclubs are. It wasn't
as big as the Palais, it probably held 400 people max. Al came out
and said everything was alright, and thanked me for bringing him
the gun.

For the next half an hour, Al whinged and moaned about
working at Chimes. I listened with half an ear, but I knew that Al
was a lunatic, and most of his problems were self-inflicted. Before
I left, he offered me a shift. I took it because I needed the money.

A few weeks later I worked a Friday night at Chimes. And what
a night it was. The earlier part of the evening was uneventful. The
punters were out to have a good time and everything was quiet.
There was just an hour or so left of the night when Beau, one of the
other doormen, said that he had to use the loo. That left me at the
front door, alone. A group of guys approached the club, and asked
to be let in. It was one o'clock and, as far as I was concerned, no-
one else was coming in.

'You're too late, the doors are shut,' I told them.

They were a motley crew, and had 'trouble', written all over
their faces. One of them piped up aggressively, 'What d'ya mean
it's too late, do yer know who I am?' He pointed to himself.

Shaking my head I told him, 'I don't care who you are, you're
not coming in'.

I had been working as a doorman for a few years now and I was
confident of my abilities. Facing a pack of violent nutcases,
wasn't daunting, in fact I thought of it as a challenge. I mentally
prepared myself to take them on. I glanced over my shoulder to
see if Beau was on his way back. He wasn't, but no problem. Out
of the corner of my eye, I saw a group of punters approach me

from inside the club. One of them seemed like a regular 'Goliath', he towered over all of us. His shaggy hair was trailing over his face.

'They're alright, they're with us. Just let 'em in,' he said gruffly.

Another person might have felt intimidated, being surrounded by a sea of men who wanted to cause trouble, but it didn't worry me. I had grown so used to violent encounters, that it was just 'all in the line of duty', as far as I was concerned.

While I was trying to reason with this guy, another of his cronies took a pop at me. His fist just caught the side of my face. Instantly, I gave him a left hook. He fell backwards. The 'Big Philistine', tried to grab me in a bear hug. I swung round quickly, and uppercut him straight on his chin. He fell down in one swoop in front of me. The one who had taken a swipe at me, began to back off. There was no way that I was going to let him off, so I jumped on the head of the guy on the floor, and vaulted out into the street. The guy who I was after, stopped and curled himself up into a ball. He knew he couldn't get away. I began to pound him mercilessly. I was so angry that he had dared to take a swing at me. All my frustration, depression and everything else bad that had happened to me, I took out on this man. He was my punchbag: I couldn't stop hitting him.

By now, the other doormen had been alerted to the trouble. Beau came up to me and said, 'C'mon now Ian, that's enough. Stop now, that's enough.'

I heard him, but I didn't want to stop. There was so much pent-up anger inside me that needed to come out, and I wanted to release it now. Eventually, Beau grabbed me. It was a good thing that he did, as the guy's face was a bloody pulp. As I had been hitting him with my bare hands, my knuckles were all busted-up and bloodied. I felt great.

The guy who had taunted me, saying, 'don't you know who I am?' was now up the road, being held back by his friends, yelling,

'You don't know who you're messing with: I'm coming back for you'.

I was feeling on top of the world and replied, 'Yeah, yeah, anytime'. Smiling at him, I slowly walked back to the club.

The feud between these guys and us continued for a few weeks. I did a few more stints at Chimes, and they did come back, but when they pulled up in their cars, we were waiting for them at the front door, so they drove off.

Al, who was the head doorman, had had enough at Chimes. He was offered a job running a pub.

'Ere Ian, 'ow do you fancy my job?' he asked me one day.

It didn't take me long to make a decision. At Top Touch I was getting about a hundred pounds for the few shifts that I did each week. At Chimes, as head doorman, I would be working most nights, and plus, I knew that whoever controlled the door, controlled the moneybag, and I knew that I could have a little scam going to boost my earnings. I said yes.

Within a fortnight of becoming the head doorman of Chimes, those guys came back, to fulfil their threats. At the time, I was having a rare evening at home, relaxing with my family. Beau's phone call, put an end to that.

'Ian, you've got to come in. Wolfy and his mates have come back with reinforcements, and they're tooled up.'

'Who's Wolfy?' I asked.

'That guy who said he would be back for you. Did you know that he stabbed some doorman at the Townhouse?'

'Why did you let them in?'

'We 'ad to, we 'ad no choice, there were loads of 'em.'

Sighing, I replaced the handset. I could have done without this aggravation, but I knew the situation had to be dealt with. So, I made a few phone calls and gathered some backup of my own. I headed for Chimes.

My car was full as I drove along the A406 towards north London. Jason was a young guy, whose body filled up most of my car. I hadn't known him for long, so I gave him a pep talk.

'Listen, mate, here's my cosh.' I handed it to him with some reluctance. I didn't know if he could handle himself, and work as part of a team. 'Make sure you use it right. I don't want to find that it's gone off, and you've kept this in your pocket.'

'No worries,' he assured me.

As I parked my car in front of the club, I could see fear and panic etched on the faces of Beau and Don at the front door. The car that was following me, spewed its occupants out. We rushed for the door.

'The place has been cleared, only the scum is left. They know you're coming.'

'C'mon, let's have 'em now.'

Inside, there were about fifteen to twenty men, gathered around the bar. As we pushed open the foyer door, the men at the bar, turned and watched as we approached them. Instantly, I recognised the guy who had promised to come back and get me. Well, he kept his word!

I knew that this situation had to be resolved. If it wasn't dealt with here and now, then that would be a signal for every nutcase in the area to come and try us out. This had to be nipped in the bud.

'Right,' I said 'let's take this outside.' I didn't want the club to get smashed up. Swaggering, they made their way outside. Wolfy, was a known local drug dealer. He obviously sampled his own wares, as his eyeballs were popping out of his head. In fact, most of his crew looked well-tanked up. This could prove to be deadly.

Taking deep breaths of night air, my mind focused on the job in hand. Don began to berate Wolfy, pointing his finger in his face: 'Now listen 'ere you . . .' Don, unfortunately, wasn't very street-wise, otherwise he would have know to hit first, and ask questions later. Wolfy got in first. He whacked Don straight on the nose. Dazed, Don staggered, clutching his face. I couldn't see if Wolfy had a 'tool' in his hand or not. I wasn't taking any chances. With my new spiky knuckle duster, I smashed him in the eye. His head shot back. But, before I had time to follow that punch with another, he retaliated and caught me straight on the nose. He was like a crazed animal. Profanities spewed out of his mouth like a geyser. My mind was whirling. I had to take this guy out quick. He was proving to be more of a problem than I had expected. I hit him three or four times in the head. Each time, the duster punctured holes in his skin, that spouted blood like a leaky hose. Finally, he collapsed in a heap. Turning the duster round to the stabbing implement, I plunged it a few times into the leather jacket he was wearing and gave him a few good kicks to his head. He didn't move.

Looking over my shoulder, I saw that the whole place was in uproar. Jason had taken my advice. He wielded the cosh like a professional. The recipient received a blow to the side of his head, which separated him from his ear! Some of Wolfy's cronies could see that they didn't have a chance against us, so they ran off.

Back in the club, we were pleased at how it had all gone. The manager looked pale and frightened, even though he had been holed up in the back of the club during the action.

'I've called the police, they'll be here any minute,' he informed us.

What a fool, I wanted to tell him that that's the last thing you do. I was just about to tell the guys to get rid of their tools, when there was a banging at the door. Looking through the glass window in the door, I could see it was Wolfy, covered in blood and gore. He looked like an extra from a horror movie! Screaming like a demented devil, he roared, 'Open up, I'm gonna have you'. Was this man indestructible? I pushed the door open, catching Wolfy unawares. He stumbled backwards. Straightening up, he stood facing us with a big blade in his hand.

'C'mon then, who's first?'

Before I could think of what to do next, one of the other guys, threw some liquid over him.

He immediately clutched his face and moaned in agony. I knew, by the smell that he had been doused with ammonia. We quickly closed the doors.

It wasn't long before bricks and stones, and any other missile they could get their hands on, came crashing through the window. My boys wanted to go outside and finish them off. I told them no. Our business now, was to hide our weapons, and wait for the police. They came, and arrested the troublemakers, finishing off the job for us. All in all, it was a good night's work.

I knew that news of this 'war' would spread around north London like wildfire. I was glad, because that meant that other troublemakers, would keep away.

Being head doorman, was good for me. My self-esteem increased and I felt more positive about myself. The large quantity of steroids that I was consuming, made me feel like Superman. The depression was held at bay, when I was working and when I trained. Although it would seep back into my life outside of those times. My goal was still intact – winning. And this time I was going to do it.

Chapter 5

DARK AND LIGHT!

The day was bright and sunny. Walking along the road I felt good – free, without a care in the world.

In an instant, the day was engulfed by blackness. Everywhere and everything was covered in darkness. 'What's happening,' I cried. I was alone, and fear gripped my heart like a vice.

The black sky cracked open and a brilliant shaft of light beamed into the darkness, swallowing it up whole. The light was blinding and I was dazed and confused. The light was powerful.

I fell down on my face – the light had a strength that I couldn't fight. I lay prostrate, unable to move. Is this the end for me?

'Ian, Ian wake up. What's wrong?' asked Val.

My heart was beating as though I had just run a hundred miles and I was drenched in sweat. The bedclothes were so wet, that if I had wrung them out, it would have filled a bucket.

I climbed out of bed and made my way to the kitchen. Valerie was behind me, asking what was wrong.

'Nah, nah nothing.'

'Well it must've been something, look at the state you're in?'

I shook my head. The frightening dreams that I had been having, were not something that I wanted to share at the moment with Val. I had had three previous. Everyone of them freaked me out. I tried to work out why it was happening to me. When I was

165

awake, my life seemed to be filled with aggravation. Nothing was going right. I had to fight to get everything. And now, I was being robbed of sleep because of these nightmares. I had never suffered from bad dreams before, why now? The dreams were bothering me. I racked my brain to think of someone who I could talk to about them. The only person I could think of was a psychiatrist, but they would probably want to lock me up. So, I tried to work out what was going on in my brain myself.

The daytime had its own worries. Through my excessive steroid consumption, I had developed gynaecomastia. Fat deposits had formed hard lumps behind the breast nipples, and they had increased in size. The pain was excruciating. My fear was that I would end up with full-blown gynaecomastia, and that my chances of competing in Japan would go out of the window. Alan had promised me that he would get me some pills which were supposed to reverse the side-effects of the drugs that had caused the problem in the first place. Each time I visited the gym Alan told me, 'I'll get them tomorrow'. But tomorrow never seemed to come. Many body builders took the drug, to combat the side effects of the steroids, but I could never lay my hands on it. I saw no point in waiting for Alan to get it for me, but I continued to take the steroids.

I now had only two weeks left in which to get the matter cleared up. I was desperate. My friend Sam advised me to come off the steroids completely.

'No way, I'm going to compete, and win, and go on to Japan,' I assured him. My determination was as strong as ever.

A week before the competition, Alan turned up with a few hundred tablets. I scoffed them down like a pig. I assumed that by taking a large number of them, they would work more quickly to reverse my problem. But there was no change at all. I was furious. 'What are these tablets, chalk?' I was disgusted. After all this time, my condition was the same. The irony was, that my body had never been in such tiptop shape as it was now: 14 stone of pure muscle. I looked good – a winner. I knew that I was by far the best I had ever been. I decided to go for it.

The South East championships were being held in Basildon. I had been dieting for a whole year. My diaries detailed every gram of food that had crossed my lips. I kept a record of every workout. The steroids that I had taken were logged. I was very serious about body building: it was my life; it was at the centre of my being. I was going to get through.

My devotion paid off. I qualified for the finals in Japan. Backstage, one of the organisers of the competition called me aside.

'Listen Ian, you were fantastic. I have no doubt that you will do well in Japan, but you have got to get that gynaecomastia sorted.'

I nodded in agreement. 'I don't know what to do, I've been taking medication, but it hasn't worked.'

'Look, take this number, and give this guy a call. He'll sort you out,' he advised.

I looked down at the piece of paper that he had written on. I knew the name of the guy.

'Yeah, I'll give him a call.' Ricardo owned a small gym in Stratford. He had been the World Champion of body building a number of years ago. He was a well respected man. I took his advice.

'I'll make arrangements for you to be operated on. Don't worry, you won't miss Japan,' he promised. 'It'll probably cost you about £500. Is that a problem?'

Shaking my head, I told him no. I was so pleased that at last I was getting the gynaecomastia treated. If I was told it was going to cost me a million pounds, somehow, somewhere, I would find the cash.

Unfortunately for me, it all fell through. I never did find out why, all I knew was that I was back to square one. Ricardo was embarrassed that despite all his careful planning I was still stuck.

'I'll tell you what Ian, let's take a drive down to the Roding Hospital, and see what they can do for you.'

I was willing to try anything.

The Roding Hospital was a private establishment. They informed me that the operation, which could be carried out within the month, would set me back £1500. I booked myself in. Now I just had to get the money.

It wasn't too difficult. I would just have to steal more money from the club. Whereas before, I worked out the money on a ratio of 2 for the club and 1 for me, it would now be 1 for the club and 2 for me. It would only be for a few weeks, and I wasn't going to let anything stand in the way of my operation. In my drug peddling, it would be easy for me to rip people off. I didn't care about anyone. My number one priority was me. I wasn't long before I got the money together. Japan, here I come, I thought optimistically.

I was due to have the operation on a Monday morning. The Friday night before, was a living nightmare, that would have far-reaching consequences.

A young woman ran from the club to the front door shouting: 'Quick, there's a fight'. Don and I charged into the club, and made our way to where the trouble was. Two young guys were going at each other hammer and tongs.

'C'mon now, break it up, break it up.'

I grabbed one guy, Don grabbed the other. As I was restraining the guy, someone shouted to me, 'Look he's got "squirt"'!'

Looking down, I saw he had a plastic bottle of nasal spray – I knew it was ammonia. This was a substance, that was easy to obtain, and it was carried around in plastic bottles. I tore the bottle out of his hand and, grabbing him by the scruff of his neck, I ran him head first through the exit door, which sprung open as the guy's head made contact with it. He flew down the steps and landed on the ground.

I shouted out: 'You're barred, and don't come back'.

I had been wanting to get rid of this guy for weeks, and now I had the perfect opportunity. Shutting the door, I felt pleased that, at last, I had seen the back of a menace.

Later that evening, though I didn't see him, I saw his handiwork. I was standing inside the club. The front door was closed. Suddenly, there was a loud banging on the door. Through the square window of the door, I saw a young woman frantically shouting and banging: 'There's some mad man smashing up a car in the car park with an axe'. The car park couldn't be seen from the front of the building. Opening the door, I charged out towards the car park. The other doormen were right behind me. A thought entered my head. Could it be my car? If it was, I would have to kill the guy. A surge of hatred welled up inside me. I ran faster. As soon as I saw my car, I roared, 'Where is he, I'm gonna kill 'im'. I ran past my car to the end of the car park. A high brick wall enclosed the car park, and I knew that this guy wasn't hiding behind it. He, wisely, had disappeared. I ran back to my car. All the windows were smashed. The axe marks were deeply imprinted in the door panels. The other doormen were saying: 'Let's kill 'im'.

Profanities were flying through the air as they expressed their outrage too. Beau shouted out, 'I think I know where he lives. Don't worry, we'll get 'im'.

Rage boiled over and gushed out of me. I wanted blood. A big tree was nearby, and I began to kick it furiously. My mood was murderous. I couldn't contain myself, so I demanded that Beau find out for me 'now' where the guy lived.

A large posse of about thirty of us, including doormen from other clubs, drove to the alleged address. The large sprawling housing estate was dimly lit. As carload after carload pulled up, people began to peep out of their windows. We found the flat that the guy was supposed to live in. We kicked the door in. Storming into the flat, we went from room to room. Each room was practically a shell. The only inhabitants were junkies, stoned out of their heads. Fear showed in their empty eyes, they knew trouble when they saw it. A young girl started to scream. I began to ask where this guy was. The junkies denied that he lived there.

'Right,' I shouted at the sad looking group. 'The next time you see 'im, tell 'im he's dead.' I meant it.

That night I got a lift home. Reluctantly, I got out of the car, and made my way to my flat. I didn't want to go home. Sleep would be a long time coming. I kept replaying in my mind, the state of my car when I first saw it. I didn't want to rest until I had dealt with the guy good and proper.

My car: how was I going to function from day to day without it? My anger dissipated and depression came to the fore. A heaviness sat on my head and shoulders. My mind became fogged: thinking was an effort. My life is cursed, I thought to myself. How could things go so dramatically wrong, and at this crucial time.

I retrieved the car the next day. Driving through the traffic was embarrassing. Every eye was on me. Other drivers and their passengers were astounded at the condition of my car, and the people in the street, stood and pointed. My eyes were focused on the road. I was hoping too, that the police wouldn't pull me up.

The mechanic that was going to repair my car, told me that it would cost in the region of £300. Shrugging, I said, 'Whatever'. I had the money put away for the operation, but I felt that somehow I could lay my hands on more money before Monday. That was, until I got home. I had been sent a letter from the hospital, with an itemised bill for the operation. What they hadn't told me at the time of giving me an estimate, was that the anaesthetist's charges had not been included. Altogether, I would now owe another £800. Shaking my head, I let defeat jump all over me. Throughout my life, I had done everything possible to achieve my goals, but now, it seemed to me that something was definitely working against me. The trouble was I couldn't see what was causing me this grief. My heart sunk lower – no Japan.

My guts wrenched and twisted as I agonised over my lost opportunity.

. . . The light was powerful. I fell down on my face – the light had a strength that I couldn't fight. I lay prostrate, unable to move. My very thoughts were exposed to the light – I was completely naked under its bright glare. Surely it was time for me to die?

I couldn't stay in bed. Life was getting so that I didn't want to be awake in the day, and I didn't want to go to sleep at night. This nightmare had recurred about four times. It was always the same. I didn't want to tell Valerie about having them. I didn't want her to think that I was weak, and couldn't handle a few scary dreams! The problem was, I didn't have anyone with whom I could talk about them. If I had tried to share my dream experiences with one of the doormen, they would have thought I had gone mad.

I sat alone, in the dark, in the front room. I was troubled. The thought did occur to me that perhaps I had gone off my head and all the bashes I had taken to my skull had now resulted in me losing my mind. A memory of a conversation I had had with my friend Marcus, Valerie's brother, came clearly back to me. We were thirteen years old. It was a cold wet night, and we were sitting in a dark alleyway, sniffing glue. We started to talk about Heaven and Hell.

'. . . I believe in Heaven and Hell. And you need to know Jesus to get to Heaven,' said Marcus, with a confidence that I put down to the glue. I was shocked and upset that Marcus was telling me, in a roundabout way, that I wouldn't be going to Heaven, because I didn't know Jesus.

'You what – what has Jesus got to do with it? Look, if you're good, you're going to Heaven, if there is such a place, and if you're bad, you're going to Hell, if there is such a place.' I wasn't too sure about what I was saying, but it made sense to me.

Marcus then arrogantly replied: 'Listen here. God has set a standard. Everybody, no matter how good they are, has fallen short of God's standard. Everyone at some point in their life, has stolen, lied, thought bad thoughts about someone, or done worse. And everyone, whether they believe in Jesus or not, is going to be held accountable for everything that they have ever said or done. Jesus, God's only son, when he was on this earth, was the only man ever to have lived who didn't do a wrong thing. Only believing in him, and receiving him as the Lord of your life, will save you from going to Hell.'

'Don't talk rubbish,' I shouted. His words had fuelled up my anger. 'You mean to tell me that my Mum is going to Hell. What kind of a God lets innocent people suffer. My Mum hasn't done anything wrong.' I was fuming.

Mockingly Marcus said: 'Get a life Ian, not only has your Mum done wrong, but so have you. And,' he continued 'so has the whole world.'

I wanted to punch his lights out when he spoke about my Mum like that. I got up and walked away from him. I glanced at him over my shoulder and thought, who does he think he is? He's got a bag of glue in his hand, sitting there, talking like a hypocrite.

From the darkness, a ray of light beamed into my mind – Marcus. That's the person who might understand what I was going through. Sleep evaded me. I sat and waited until the first light of day, and then I called him.

What he told me wasn't what I wanted to hear. Boldly, Marcus said, 'Ian, Jesus is calling you. He is the light . . .'

I didn't give him a chance to go on. I said, 'Look Marcus, I don't want to hear all that. I just want the dreams to stop. I've got enough problems in my life. I haven't got time to get religious.'

'Okay mate, I hear you,' he replied. 'But, if you have another dream, call out to Jesus and ask him into your life. Believe me, after that your dreams will stop.'

'I don't know about Jesus coming into my life, but I definitely want the dreams to stop.'

The conversation that I had with Marcus, didn't make me feel any better. I tried to think of someone else who might be able to help me. My wife? But, as she was Marcus' sister and had had the same kind of upbringing, I knew it would be a waste of time telling her.

My wife went to church periodically. We had reached an agreement years before, that I wouldn't talk about violence, and she wouldn't discuss God. I wanted to keep to that.

A few nights later I had another dream – with a variation at the end:

. . . I fell down on my face – the light had a strength that I couldn't fight. I lay prostrate, unable to move.

Suddenly, I was standing up. My feet moved as I walked in the direction of a city. The bright light was behind me, following where I was going. Approaching the city, I first saw people going about their business. On closer inspection, I saw that the people didn't have any eyes. Fear gripped me, I didn't want to go further. But something evil, like a force was pulling me closer and closer, to the city. I tried to resist, but the evil force was stronger than me.

I heard a warm, loving voice behind me, yet at the same time, inside me say: 'This is where you're going Ian, unless you call on me.'

I woke up. Petrified, and shaken by the dream, I woke Valerie up. I no longer cared how I looked to her. I needed help. I could no longer hold back the tears.

'Val, I've had a terrible dream.'

Sleepily, she asked me about it. When I had finished she said, 'Ian, let's pray and ask Jesus to take away these dreams and ask him to come into your life.'

'C'mon let's do it now,' I replied desperately. At that point, I would have done anything to be free of those nightmares. The funny thing was, after we had prayed I felt peaceful. A calmness settled on me which replaced the fear. I slept like a baby.

For the next few days, I kept wondering if that short prayer that I had prayed with my wife could really make me into a Christian?

I wasn't, surely? Looking in the mirror, I appeared to be the same. And deep down, my emotions and attitudes were the same. Yet, every now and again I would think about God. Could he be real? Who was Jesus? What did it mean, that he was the Son of God? Mental pictures of him on the cross, would seep into my mind, and I would stop what I was doing to ponder upon them. We had been given a Bible as a wedding present. I tried to read it, but it didn't seem to make much sense, although the stories about Jesus were interesting.

Depression still hung around my neck like a noose. My dream of becoming World Champion seemed to be so far out of my reach. The gynaecomastia was still a problem and raising the money for the operation was proving to be difficult. My job at Chimes was becoming very violent. Every night I was fighting and beating people up. I enjoyed every punch and kick, and whatever else I could do to inflict harm upon someone.

One night, the violence escalated out of control. This particular night, the violence had erupted into a mini war. Blood flowed like a river. The police came. They arrested all the doormen, including me. I spent a miserable weekend banged up in a police cell. They questioned me relentlessly about the incident. At one point, in the break from being interviewed by the police, I laid on the bed, after counting all the specks on the ceiling, and walking up and down the little cell. I wondered why, even after praying that prayer with Valerie, my life seemed to be out of control. Since that prayer, I had tried to be good, in my own strength. Yet, I wasn't making it: I had gone in completely the opposite direction and was even worse than I had been before. My mind was jumping all over the place. I reasoned that if God knew everything, and he knew that I was trying hard to get on the right side of him, why had I ended up in this predicament? Why had he let my life go so wrong? Did he really have the power to help me? All the training I had done, in the last five or six years, was for nothing. I had not been able to go on to compete in a major competition, due to unforeseen circumstances. Where was God in all of that?

The outcome of my arrest was, that I was charged with violence and disorder. It carried a five year plus imprisonment, if found guilty. But having this charge hanging over my head didn't deter me from my violent behaviour.

A couple of months later, I was embroiled in more violent activities. Another big fight broke out in Chimes. We doormen steamed in. We grabbed bodies, and threw them out of the exit door. Nearly everyone got a slap or punch, to help them on their way. Twenty minutes later, a loud bang was heard outside the building. Rushing to see what was happening, we charged out of the door and round to the side of the building.

One of the guys we had thrown out, had made a Molotov cocktail and had pitched it against the side of the club. It hadn't exploded, but, he had another ready in his hand. He threw it towards the club. I didn't wait to see what was happening, I just charged at him. He stood facing me. I shouted, 'What do you think you're doing?'

He replied cockily, 'Nothing'.

He was over six foot tall. I glanced behind him, and saw that his mates were filling up more bottles from the petrol station.

'Nothing?' I yelled at him, punching him straight on his jaw. He fell backwards, and crashed to the floor, so I kicked him a few times. Another doorman, punched him while he was on the floor. The guy was now unconscious. John, another doorman, was beating a guy with his cosh. I shouted to all the doormen: 'Let's get back inside, before the Old Bill come'. With a few last kicks and punches, we retreated back into the club.

We had a few drinks, and a laugh and joke about the fight.

'Ian you knocked the geezer out with one punch, you are bad man,' laughed one of the doormen. I felt proud hearing the comments from the guys. The fact that they had seen me in action, looking good, made me feel a bit better about myself.

Driving home alone, I replayed the fight again in my mind. Proud and boastful feelings were suddenly replaced with guilt. This was a feeling that I had rarely, if ever experienced before, particularly in association with my work. I began to argue with myself: 'The geezer deserved what I gave him, he was taking liberties'. But, another thought entered my head: 'You shouldn't have hit him'. Pangs of guilt flashed through my mind and it was hard to shift them. 'I was just doing my job,' I reasoned with myself.

I pulled over into a lay-by, on the A406. I had to take hold of my mind. I couldn't while I was driving. I needed to think about these new thoughts. As I was sitting alone in the car, a voice, although inaudible, was speaking into me.

'You've done something wrong.'

I kept reasoning, and arguing, and wrestling with myself about the incident earlier. Then, thoughts of other situations came into my mind. And slowly, like the breaking of day, I began to realise that I truly had done wrong. In fact, all of my life, I had been living by the wrong values. What Marcus had told me was true. I could feel the essence of the truth deep inside of me. No-one had to tell me, 'Ian you're wrong'. For the first time in my life, I now grasped the fact that I was in the wrong. That truth hit me like a sledgehammer. Not only was the violence wrong, but everything I did was not right. I don't know how I knew, but believe me, I knew. I thought about the times I had used the name of Jesus as a swear word, and I literally cringed. The shame of what I had said covered me. I felt very unclean – dirty. From childhood, I had been surrounded by people swearing and behaving in a questionable manner, and it had never worried me – until now.

Leaning back against the seat, I felt terrible. Never had anyone or anything invoked such emotions in me, which caused me to become aware of myself.

I cried out: 'Jesus, if you're real help me, change me, take away this filth from my life. Forgive me Jesus.'

A tingle erupted over my body. What was happening to me? A warmth slowly entered my heart, and the power of it, cracked open my heart, which seemed like a stone. The thick darkness, and evil that had dominated my heart, seemed to seep out, as this other power, which I can only describe as a strong love, filled me up. After a while, I felt clean. It was like when a torrent of rain cascades down, and then after it has passed, everywhere looks bright and clean. That was me. Clean. Tears streamed down my face, I couldn't control myself: I was weeping like a baby.

The strange thing was, I assumed at the time, that it was me just coming to an understanding of the reality of how I had been living and that I could now see things differently. It happened so naturally, without human intervention, that it was hard to imagine that it was all down to Jesus. In the matter of an hour or so, I had come to know that Jesus was real, he was alive. What I had experienced, wasn't a figment of my imagination, I had actually gone through something. Jesus was spiritually tangible to me. Before such a time, I didn't even know that I possessed a spirit. Now, I was sure that I had one. Truly, as I drove off, I knew that that experience in the lay-by had changed me – forever. I was a new Ian McDowall.

Looking back, I wouldn't have recognised myself. I no longer swore; profanities were a thing of the past. The violence and anger had evaporated, and in their place was a calmness.

My desire to know God more, increased daily. I bought a Bible, and I started to attend a church in Canning Town, east London. The doormen that I worked with, all knew about the change in my life.

They laughed, 'Oh Ian, you've seen the light.'

I didn't care. What I had was real, and I wasn't ashamed of it.

My love for my wife and daughter changed too. The selfish ambitions that had prevented me from making room for a deep love for anyone else, was now replaced with something stronger and more real.

Steve Jamison, a member of the church in Canning Town invited Valerie and I to have some lunch with his family.

'. . . What was the worst thing about you, before you became a Christian?' asked Steve. For a minute I paused. The violent acts, and drug-taking went through my mind, and then I stopped on body building.

'Body building,' I said with much conviction. As I spoke, it was like a new revelation to me.

'I have always wanted to do something with my life, and when I got into body building, I thought I had arrived. It completely took over my life. I would eat, think, and sleep body building. I would've given up everything to become a champion. My obsession with body building was such, that it was god to me.' I surprised myself by what I said next.

'And do you know what Steve, if I had an opportunity to get rid of my gynaecomastia, I would never compete again.' I meant every word of it.

That was Sunday afternoon. On Monday morning, I was put to the test. A letter arrived from the hospital in Billericay to say that an appointment had been made available for me, on the National Health Service to remove the gynaecomastia. I was shocked. I wasn't even aware that my name was on the waiting list. Apparently, the surgeon who was going to perform the operation at the private hospital, when I didn't turn up, had put my name on the NHS list. I knew that Jesus was offering me a way out. With the letter in my hand, I prayed to the Lord, and thanked him for his provision. I promised, there and then, that I would never compete again. My desire for body building had gone.

People around me have been amazed at how, through the years, I have clung on to Jesus. Since that time, even though I haven't deserved a thing, God's presence in my life has been more than positive. The anger that was always part of me, has been replaced by love. Not just a love that someone would have for a friend, but something that is rooted deep within my being.

Materially, physically, and especially spiritually, my life has changed for the better. Yes, at times, things go wrong, and I feel a bit stressed. But, nothing like how I used to feel. My selfish ambition which said, 'I want to be somebody, I want to win' – me, me, me, is no longer me. Now, my life is focused on the important things in my life. Family, friends and work are essentials that need my time and energy. But now, Jesus is the God of my life, and not me.

TOUGH TALK

'. . . Coke was my life. My heart was ballooning into the size of a small football. I was slowly killing myself with my addiction. I realised that I would be dead soon – I needed help. The truth is that Jesus set me free, and he can set you free!' Arthur's voice boomed out across the packed church. Behind him, on the main stage the rest of the guys had finished lifting weights, and were setting up the equipment for Arthur to use. Fifteen hundred faces appeared transfixed, as each member of the 'Tough Talk' team spoke in turn, about their relationship with Christ, and the need for everyone present, if they hadn't done so already, to make the decision to give their life to him too. A flood of people responded.

Christ Tabernacle is a large multi-racial church in Queens, New York. It is the second largest church in New York, and the sister church of the famous Brooklyn Tabernacle. Arthur, Steve and Ian, as they prayed for the people that had come forward, were each overwhelmed by the fact that God had chosen them to share his Gospel in such a unique way.

As the bus, that carried the team and their gear, drove through the busy New York streets to their next meeting, Arthur's mind went back over the few years since he had become a Christian. Life for him had changed beyond recognition.

'You've lost it, you've completely lost it,' said Vic.

Swallowing deeply, I repeated myself: 'My children bought me a Bible, and my wife bought me a tambourine for Father's Day.'

Roars of laughter resounded around the warehouse. I had gone in to work at 2 a.m. The shift had begun as usual, with a mug of tea. Sipping my brew, I could understand why the guys had responded the way they did. Most people who had known me before I became a Christian, tended to receive the information the same way. These folk had known me as a drug-taking, knife-wielding, violent man. Now, I had done a 180° turn around, and they were finding it hard to believe. This was the start of the ridicule that has continued to follow me.

Nowadays, I tell people that I still use the Bible, but the tambourine has gone into retirement! It was amazing to think that prior to becoming a Christian, no-one in their right mind would have dared laugh at me. My reaction, if they had, would have been very different.

I continued to work at Spitalfields market for about two years, after I made a commitment to Christ. It was tough because, although I had changed, the environment around me was just as crazy. Drugs were readily available, and the people that were around me were taking them just the same. People still approached me to ask me to collect money that was owed them, and violence was a daily occurrence, although I no longer participated. What kept me strong in this environment, was my new found faith, prayer and reading the Bible. At the age of 42, I found new friends within the church, who gave me support, advice, and helped me to get through those difficult days.

After telling my story at my church, I got invited to various meetings to tell people about what had happened to me. The Full Gospel Business Men's Fellowship International (FGBMFI) asked me to speak at one of their dinners and this led to further engagements up and down the country. However, as a lone voice, there were occasions when I struggled. At an FGBMFI breakfast, where I was a guest, I met up with Ian. I realised during our conversation, that Ian and I had a lot in common, and we formed a friendship.

Ian asked me to come along with him and a group of guys to speak at a prison. It was then that Ian explained to me about Tough Talk. Basically, it was a group of men with similar backgrounds, who had come to know the reality of Jesus Christ. I felt comfortable with these guys, and hoped that I could work with them again in the future.

It seemed incredible that, since 1998, I had travelled all over Britain, and now was in the United States of America, and all this had come about through Tough Talk.

The bus ground to a halt outside the Hosanna Church in Spanish Harlem. The building was well-kept and neat, in sharp contrast to the surrounding area. As the guys were unloading the bus, waiting for the church to open, Steve and Ian decided it was time for food.

Walking down the road, the local people stopped to watch the guys pass by. They stood out – maybe it was their east London swagger, or perhaps it was the clothes they were wearing. Whatever the reason, they were curious. Four hundred yards later, they found themselves inside a deli. At the checkout, the cashier enquired about the food Steve had purchased.

The Chinese American asked with a Spanish accent: 'What food have you in those bags?'

I replied, 'Two 'am rolls, an' two cheese rolls luv'.

She looked at me puzzled, and said, 'Sorry, can you repeat that?'

I said, 'Yeah, two 'am rolls, an' two cheese rolls luv'.

Confusion spread rapidly across her face: 'Sorry sir, have you any English?'

'English what?'

'Sorry, do you speak English?'

I said, 'Excuse me darlin', I am English. I've got two 'am rolls, an' two cheese rolls.'

She started to speak very slowly, saying, 'I'm sorry, I can't understand anything you are saying, I don't know what language you are speaking', and with that she called for help. Looking over my shoulder, I glanced at Ian, who was creasing up with laughter.

Standing in the deli, thousands of miles away from home, in this comical situation, where this young woman could not understand my English, made me take stock of why I was there and where I had come from. It took me back to the day that I first met Ian. I know now, that he was the man who had given me my first Bible, long before I became a Christian, on the day I was planning a violent act. A year later, I gave my life to Jesus, and called Ian to let him know. He did not remember me at first, but when I mentioned the Bible, he knew who I was.

' . . . So how has being a Christian changed your life Steve?'

I laughed. So many different thoughts flashed through my mind. When I first met Ian, in the office of Alan's gym, I was on my way to get drunk. I was still trying to take it in, that drinking no longer formed any part of my life.

'Well, the thing is Ian, I'm just about to buy a house.'

'Oh right, you're leaving the estate. Buying a house is going to set you back a few quid.'

'It's amazing really. The money that I used to spend on booze, will be paying my mortgage.'

'If you're not spending time in the pub with your mates, what are you doing? And what has happened to your drinking pals?'

'It's funny really, a lot of the really dodgy ones seem to have disappeared. I've just done an Alpha Course at church, and I've really thrown myself into church activities, and people have been asking me to come and talk about my life at their church.'

Ian asked me whether I still had a desire for alcohol.

'I can take it or leave it. Gone are the seven nights a week up the pub. Drink rarely passes my lips, I now never feel the urge to drink. I'm no longer addicted to that crazy lifestyle.'

'What about your wife and family, how are they coping with the change?'

'Lisa thought I was mad at first, but six weeks later, she too became a Christian.'

'That's fantastic Steve, and you're even sharing your story. What are you doing next Sunday?'

'Not much, why do you ask?'

'Because I'm visiting a prison and I'd like you to come with me . . .'

The rest is history. Tough Talk has become a large part of my life since that telephone conversation.

Being in New York, waiting to speak at another church, was just another unbelievable experience that had occurred in my life since I had become a Christian.

'Boarding now at gate 27 for London Heathrow, is flight number V009.' The Tough Talk group slowly made their way to the plane. The flight take off was smooth. Ian settled into his seat, and glanced around at the team and their families. As his attention went from Arthur to Steve, Adam McMillian and John Burns and the other members of Tough Talk, he was amazed by the way God had brought them all together, and was using them in such a dynamic way.

Door work was still a struggle for me when I was a young Christian. I was wrestling with my new found faith, and trying to keep out of the way of violent encounters. No longer carrying weapons on me, I now had to handle situations differently.

One night, a guy outside the nightclub where I was working, became threatening and abusive. We would not let him into the club. He began to push me and shout at me. I tried to ignore him, but the more he went on at me, the harder it was becoming to control myself. Instinctively, I hit him, 'wham', in the face. He fell backwards down the porch stairs. Straight away, I regretted what I had done. I glanced at the doorman that I was working with. His look spoke volumes. I had been telling this guy about Jesus, week in and week out. I was so full of what God had done for me and how Jesus had changed me – but now, I had blown it.

The week that followed was one of deep soul searching. I was riddled with guilt and shame. I felt that the guys would no longer take me seriously, because of what I had done. But God has a way of making something good come out of something bad. The next week came, and I was doing the same shift at the nightclub. The guy I had hit turned up again, with a hammer! He was banging it against the front wall of the club, pointing his finger at me, shouting, 'You're gonna get this mate'.

I walked out towards him. Instead of the usual feeling of mounting aggression, that would rise up inside me, with each step I was taking, a calmness seemed to flood the inside of me. Out of the corner of my eye, I noticed a couple of doormen running round the back of him, to grab him.

'Get back inside, leave this to me,' I shouted to them.

To my surprise, they did.

Alone with this guy, I began to talk to him. I can only say that it was the peace of God that calmed this guy down. One minute, he was a raving lunatic wielding a hammer, the next, he seemed like a rational, sensible man. A few minutes later, we were shaking hands! God graciously enabled me to put right the wrong I had done the man the week before. In fact, one of the doormen became a Christian a few weeks later.

A few of the men I worked with also became born-again Christians. One night, I was asked by the leader of my church, Steve Derbyshire, if I would like to share my life story. To my surprise, he also asked me to bring some weights. That Sunday evening, after I had performed some powerlifting demonstrations and told my life story, several people, including an old lady, came forward, when the congregation were asked if there was anyone who wanted to give their life to Jesus. I felt so encouraged that my life story had affected this old lady, that I knew, given the chance, many more people could be affected.

Tough Talk has evolved over the last five years. In 1996, we were invited to speak at a church called The Powerhouse, in Wood

Green, North London. When we arrived that evening, they had put some posters up advertising us. They called the evening 'Tough Talk'. The name has stuck ever since.

The memories of the early years of Tough Talk filled my mind, as the plane took us back to England. I thanked God that He brought an ordinary bunch of guys from the east end of London together, travelling the world, sharing in so many wonderful places and with so many people, what He has done in our lives as individuals and collectively. I know that He still has much for us to do.

* * *

Tough Talk is now a charitable trust. Our aim is solely to share with people what God has done for us all. We are not preachers or teachers, just men who have come to know the reality of the living God, through Jesus Christ, His son.

If this book has touched you in some way, and you would like to invite Jesus Christ into your life, here is a simple prayer you can pray:

> Dear Lord, I am sorry for the wrong things I have done in my life. I believe that the Lord Jesus died on the cross for me, and took away my sins. I believe that he rose from the dead, and is alive today. Please forgive me and come into my life. Thank you Jesus. Amen.

After reading these stories of lives changed so incredibly, you may feel that you would like to know more about Jesus. If so, you can contact Tough Talk at their e-mail address or by post and they will send you further information and an address of a local Church or Christian group meeting near you.

Tough Talk are a group of guys who travel the UK, Europe and the USA, performing powerlifting demonstrations as a back-drop, while telling their astonishing stories. If you would like to book Tough Talk to come to your church, school or prison, simply e-mail or write to them at the address below.

Tough Talk is a registered charity and requests no fees. Members of Tough Talk take no income from sharing their faith, therefore, any gifts of money received go directly to the charity, whose purpose is advancing the Christian faith. Should you wish to find out more about Tough Talk's activities, please contact them at the address below.

Tough Talk
119 George Lane
South Woodford
London
E18 1AN

E-mail: Toughtalk1@aol.com
Tel: 07000 777 270
Fax: 07000 782 059